Antiques Don't Lie

Antiques Don't Lie

HOW TO MAKE ANTIQUE FURNITURE TELL
EVERYTHING, INCLUDING ITS AGE

Nelson E. Way
and Constance Stapleton

DOUBLEDAY & COMPANY, INC.
GARDEN CITY, NEW YORK
1975

Library of Congress Cataloging in Publication Data

Way, Nelson E   1908–
Antiques don't lie

1. Furniture—Expertising.   2. Furniture—
Collectors and collecting.   I. Stapleton, Constance, 1930–
joint author.   II. Title.
NK2240.W37   749   ISBN 0-358-07087-X
Library of Congress Catalog Card Number 74–33083

Contents

CONTENTS

Introduction

Do you realize that anyone, given a simple set of clues, can make an antique sit up and talk?

It's true. Antiques don't lie. They can't. If you know what to look for, you can find out how old a piece of furniture is, where and how it was made and much of what has happened to it since.

Yet of the volumes written on antiques, not one discusses this in easy-to-follow terms that a novice can understand. There are books on makers, periods, regions, woods, chairs and prices, but not one that shows you how to examine an antique the way an expert does.

As a consequence, many beginners resort to price guides. This is a good beginning, but as your eye improves, you realize that the rarest, one-of-a-kind antiques are seldom catalogued. They pass on the auction block disguised by only a thin coat of paint, go for pennies at farmers' auctions and at secondhand prices in consignment shops.

The only secret is in knowing what to look for.

Antiques don't lie, but sellers sometimes do, either for

money's sake or from sheer ignorance. A family selling Grandma's treasures may only know what she told them. The price is often too high and the treasure too young.

Visit any antique shop and the most frequently heard question is "How old is it?" This question leaves the buyer wide open for answers like "post-Civil War" (early 1930s), "primitive" (it was hacked out of an old orange crate yesterday), or "in the Chippendale style" (anything with ball and claw feet). Some dealers don't like to say "I don't know." If you find one who does, go back and visit him often. He's honest and a great friend to have.

Ask questions. The more you ask, the more you will learn. The easiest and best place to start is "What do you know about the piece?" This gives the seller room to say anything that comes into his head without telling him how much you know. Follow this with "Where did it come from?" or "What kind of wood is it?" and you're well on your way.

The answers can clue you in to a world of bargains. Recently, when a dealer called to say she had a set of Queen Anne chairs, we asked the recommended questions and learned: "I bought them in England. They look like mahogany, but my husband says they're maple."

After you've finished reading this book, that last word should set off every alarm in your head. Maple is not an English wood. A quick trip to her shop proved our suspicions. The chairs were actually American, worth many times her asking price and an absolute steal (which we did).

INTRODUCTION

The more you look, the more you will develop a feeling for style. That's what antique hunting is all about. If you don't recognize styles, visit your local library, museum, historical society or the best antique dealer in town.

Why the best? Because unlike other fields, the best place to start in antiques is at the top. The reason for this, while not always obvious to the novice, is honesty. Good dealers don't have to exaggerate to make a sale. In fact, no sale is worth their integrity. While learning from the best teachers, you have an opportunity to examine the finest antiques firsthand. Ask questions. Admit when you don't know something and you'll learn more. Pretend that you know and if a dealer is the least bit dishonest, he'll know what he can get away with.

Study old paintings of other periods. Background furniture is often painted more exactly than today's illustrations and photography can duplicate it.

Go to antique shows. Dealers who work shows often specialize. You'll see the most and best of many things you didn't even know were antiques and get expert direction while you learn.

Before long, you'll be able to spot the difference between an exception to the rule and outright fakery.

Acquiring antiques is an art, a practice in patience, an absorbing game and a rewarding hobby that can pay higher dividends than the stock market.

Anyone can play . . . and often does. You don't need a license to join or a degree to succeed.

All you have to do is decide to begin.

Antiques Don't Lie

CHAPTER 1

Approach

This chapter should really be entitled "Begin," but then it would have to be placed after "Backs" and "Beds," which is definitely not the place to start.

You will need a kit. Begin with a few items if the accumulation embarrasses you, but you will find, as your expertise grows, that you need them all.

Measuring tape (If you're clever and can multiply, measure your hand span. If we had been able to master the No. 8 multiplication table, we could leave the measuring tape at home.)

Pocket-size flashlight (to see under, behind and beneath)

Screwdriver (to unscrew screws when no one is looking)

Small magnifying glass (to examine screw threads and other markings more closely)

Calipers (to measure diameter. With age, wood shrinks and becomes oval, a state of age most difficult to reproduce, especially on turnings.)

Small penknife or razor blade (this will send shudders down the spine of every dealer, but if every square inch is painted, there is no other way short of infrared film to know what is underneath. But please . . . scrape only where it won't show.)

You are now ready to stalk the game. Try not to ask questions about a piece until you have first examined it.

Stand back and see what it says to you. Is it balanced? Does it look like all its pieces began life together? Is it all one kind of wood? (See "Woods," Chapter 39.) One style? (Chapter 35) If something has been added from another period, why? Is there a balance to the piece, a continuity of style? Does the color look right? Is it too short? Does it look like the top or bottom of something else?

Now walk over to the piece. Feel it, smell it. Open its parts. As you examine each section, write down the approximate age of that part. After a thorough examination, these dates should be in the same ball park. If there is a discrepancy, check that particular chapter to find out what it means.

For instance, if the drawers are old, but the back isn't, the piece may have been built around old store drawers. If you're sure the feet have been replaced, see "Feet," Chapter 16.

The chapters in this book are arranged for easy reference because antiques don't have the same parts. Some chapters do not have as many dates listed (i.e., "Bottoms"), but you must know what to look for in these areas in order to determine the authenticity of the whole. Where there is only one date listed rather than a time span, that is the earliest date.

If you want to save time, we suggest the following order: Observe carefully. If it looks good, then try to find something wrong with it. Start with the front, pull out a drawer or door. Look at the interior, the joinings, the back, the feet, the bottom and the glue blocks. Add up the total.

In a very short time, you will know what to look for without checking each chapter. Soon, you'll be leaving your book at home. Before long, you will become so expert that when you go to auctions, people will take up all your time asking you how old something is.

We know. That's why we wrote this book.

CHAPTER 2

Backs

Don't ever pass up a back. It can either prove your suspicions are true or be the clincher for authenticating a good piece.

Backs are left unfinished; therefore, it is an excellent place to read the history of an antique to see what conditions it has endured and find out what changes have been made to it structurally.

It doesn't matter if the boards run vertically or horizontally. It's how they feel that counts. Run your hand over the boards (see "Feel," Chapter 15). Do they feel ripply to the touch, thicker in the middle than at the sides? If so, they are hand planed and early. If they feel rough but flat, check for saw marks.

If you see circular markings (arched grooves), the boards were cut by a circular saw and the piece was made *after* 1850. If the boards show a checkered houndstooth pattern, they were cut with a straight saw and the piece was made *before* 1850.

How wide are the boards? Years ago there were many large trees and workmen could afford to use big fat boards in the back of a piece. As our country grew and the supply of large trees diminished, backboards became narrower. The wider the board, the older the piece.

How thick are the boards? If a full inch thick (rather than a fraction under), it is a sign of an early individually made piece. Modern boards, when dressed, are not a full inch thick. If the boards are thin, about one-fourth-inch thick and feel smooth and flat, they are machine planed and the piece has been made since 1870. Is the back all one piece of wood that looks like fiber board or plywood? If so, check all other sections very carefully. Plywood was not invented until 1900. It may be a well-made reproduction.

Look for spaces between the boards. Because age shrinks wood across the grain, backboards on old pieces usually pull apart.

What kind of wood is the back made of? Old pieces usually have backs made of poplar because it was easy to work with and inexpensive to use. Poplar has a uniform

4

color with a green or yellow tinge (green came from the outer part of the tree, while yellow came from the inner). A few old pieces have pine backs. To recognize the difference, check the grain. With age, poplar becomes pitted (like a peach pit) whereas pine grows into valleys and peaks (similar to barn siding).

How are the boards joined together? (See "Joining," Chapter 20.) Although backboards are usually only butted together, there are exceptions. In good early pieces, the backboards were chamfered together to keep the interior dust free. This means one edge was made thinner in order to fit into the next board. This form of construction dates from 1750 to 1850.

Tongue and groove construction was used on some backs from 1725 to 1850 to keep interiors free from dust.

How are the backboards joined to the main section? Some early backs were joined with wooden pegs because nails were expensive. If you see this on a piece, the chances are it was made before the Revolutionary War.

Early nails cannot always be an indication of age because they were saved and reused, but if everything else checks out, they are a plus factor. If the majority of the nails on the back are mushroom or rosebud heads and all else adds up, you have a rare piece.

However, if there are nail holes without nails, or the nails are different kinds, it may be an indication something has been done to the piece.

If the antique has more than one section i.e., chest-on-chest, cupboard or highboy), make sure all backboards are the same color. They may be light or dark, but should be even. The upper part should be the exact shade as the bottom. If it is not, the pieces did not go together originally and are "married." If it is not a good match, it is referred to in the trade as "bastardized."

Are the ends of the backboards the same color as the back? If not, this signifies one of two things: A new back was cut from old boards, or the piece was cut down from something else.

What if a back is painted or stained? Watch out! This may be an indication alterations have been made and covered up. Check all other sections carefully.

See also: Chapters on "Feel," "Joining," "Nails," "Screws," "Woods."

CHAPTER 3

Beds

It is estimated that there were twelve times as many chairs made as beds. Beds were well used, sometimes kept in the main room and often used by more than one person.

Early beds were shorter in length because people were shorter. Prior to 1860, beds were made to order. They were simple in style, relying on draperies for effect. Sometimes only the footposts were turned to save time and money. Prior to 1730, there was often no footboard. The bed was the mattress; the frame, the bedstead.

Early beds are usually marked with Roman numerals I through VIII, cut with a chisel on each section. If you see these numerals, make sure they have been cut by the same hand and are all the same size and style. This is a good way to determine if all parts are original or discover which have been replaced.

Look in the mortises of rails for dirt, dust and the handcrafted marks of age. This is one place fakers usually forget to fake.

Measure bedposts with a caliper. Wood shrinks with age, becoming oval rather than round. Kiln-dried wood doesn't shrink in this way.

Posts should be three inches in diameter at the square part where the rails are inserted. Cut-down ones are often only two inches. Until 1825, the style of beds remained much the same since Pilgrim days, although fine high post bed-steads of Queen Anne style (1710–35) were found in the United States. From 1735 on, beds grew in quality as homes improved.

Exceptions: Rope beds (with pegs or holes six to ten inches apart, through which rope was woven to support the mattress) are associated with the earlier 1800s, but were made as late as 1900. Iron catches (that replaced the earlier wood mortise and tenon joints) are associated with the late 1800s, but were invented as early as 1820.

Sometimes beds have been made into something else like a garden seat or sofa. Since older side rails usually have to be replaced with longer sections to accommodate today's regulation-size mattresses, it is a relatively simple matter to remake the piece as a bed.

1600 on

Trundle bed. Fifteen inches high, kept under another bed during the day to save space and slide out at night to accommodate extra people, or used for children.

1600s on

Day bed. Long chair with six legs used in living room. Kept small for easy moving. Style and period determined by back, feet and joinings. Some japanned. Recamier or Grecian sofa later styles with curving back and long armrest on one side.

1690–1775

Under-the-eaves bed. Another space-saving device with short headpost. Made of pine or birch with maple posts. Ash is rare.

Mid-1770s

Chippendale beds grow to seven or eight feet in height. English and American beds differ in the shape of the posts. English posts usually have the same diameter top and bottom, while American posts are tapered.

1730–1835

High post bed with two or four posts supporting tester.

1750–80

Pencil posts. Thin six-sided posts. The thinner the post, the better the bed.

1760 on

Low post bed with Chippendale legs.

Late 1700s to early 1800s

Field bed gains in popularity around Philadelphia. Arched frame with curved canopy. Also called a tent bed. Style originated in Crusades. Could be taken apart and moved easily.

1785–95

Hepplewhite style, 6 feet to 8½ feet. High reeded posts, square leg with spade foot. American beds have metal decorations on bolt covers. This feature is seldom found on English beds.

1800–50

Settee bed. Sofalike frame on legs expands outward to sleep two people. When closed, it looks like a deacon bench. Settle or bench beds with a boxlike bottom are Canadian.

1810–40

Sheraton-style scroll or roll-over top headboard. Carving

becomes more impressive. Posts less tapered, with more carving and turnings. Rope lacings used instead of springs. Wheels or casters are added to feet to facilitate moving. Sheraton invents the summer bed, two beds under one canopy.

1815–80

Spool turnings (also called Jenny Lind). Earlier versions have handmade turnings. Mass produced from 1850 on have more uniform turnings.

1820

Invention of iron catch hook that slides into post, replacing mortise and tenon joint found in earlier beds.

1820–60

Low poster bed 3 feet 6 inches to 4 feet 2 inches high, with all posts the same height. Balls or turnings for feet.

1825 on

Heavy leaf or pineapple carving.

1830

First use of slats to replace rope. Countersunk screws appear.

1840 on

Empire period. Twin beds appear on the scene. Heavy, darker, spiral carvings. Heavily carved leafage, spirals or rings, sometimes gilded or painted black. Boat and gondola shapes. Screws and plate replace mortise and tenon joints. Mahogany, cherry, maple or birch woods.

1840–50

Sleigh bed. Usually mahogany veneer or rosewood.

1840–65

Half tester bed popular in South. High headboard with cartouche, space in tester frame inset with silk or satin. Made of mahogany or mahogany with rosewood.

1840–65

Three-fourths high posts with steeple finials. All posts same height, plain or paneled headboard or ten short spool or baluster-turned spindles.

High post beds made during this period have wooden cornice, chunkier in style than earlier testers.

1840–75

Gothic influence. Panels and arches, mahogany or black walnut with burl veneer. Cast-iron catches fastening side rails to head and foot.

1845–60

Round corners. Belter and Louis XV low beds.

1860–1910

Cast-iron beds come into vogue as cast-iron garden furniture gains in popularity. Often mold contains name of maker and date of manufacture. If date is not included look in city directory, local library or historical archives to ascertain dates manufacturer was in business.

1865–75

Horizontal panels, carved central decoration of grapes with tendrils or fruit, nuts and flowers. Walnut, ash. Carvings and molding black walnut.

Painted cottage bed appears in simpler version with painted scenes or flowers in place of carvings. Painted to resemble black walnut.

1865–80

Renaissance period. Rounded corners, heavy in appearance, deep elaborate panels with beveled edges. Crestlike carvings. Black walnut.

1875 on

Late Victorian. Towering carved headboards with raised panels, factory produced. Black walnut or ash trimmed with black walnut. Carvings and moldings made separately and glued to the surface.

1870–80

Eastlake painted bed, similar but simpler version of above, painted in yellow and brown tones with painted scenes or flowers. Pine, maple.

1870–90

Eastlake paneled bed. Straight topped foot and headboard

with square and rectangular panels. Flat overhanging top rail with carving underneath. Simple curved lines with geometric scrolls and designs.

1880 on
Brass beds.

CHAPTER 4

Brasses, Handles, Escutcheons

If brasses (or pulls) have not been replaced, they can be used to determine the age of a piece.

To see if they are original, examine the front and inside of the drawer for evidence of previous pulls. Do you see markings of other designs or holes that have been filled? Wear from a drop pull or a cotter pin? (A cotter pin looks like a sprung bobby pin and leaves the imprint of a wide V on the inside of the drawer.)

Very early brasses, drop handles and other hardware were attached with cotter pins held in place by iron wire, bent at a right angle and then driven into the wood. Very few pieces survive with this type of pull intact because it was held in place by a single fastener and not strong enough for daily use. However, if you find indications that the drawer once had a single fastener, you can date the piece from 1660 to 1720.

Prior to 1750, brasses were light in color because of a high content of zinc and tin. From 1750 on, brass became darker as copper was added to the content. After 1750, some brasses also had gilded surfaces which wore through, producing double tones.

Do the handles match the escutcheons? (Escutcheons are the brass keyhole plates.) Handles often wore out with age or were replaced to keep up with the styles. Escutcheons were not easy to replace. Therefore, if the handles and escutcheons do not match, date the piece by the escutcheons.

Check the back of the bail handle for a signature or maker's name. If you find one, look it up in a directory of makers to ascertain the exact date of manufacture. If you discover it is an English maker, this does not mean that it is an English piece. Brass was imported by America until the Revolutionary War, and all of Hepplewhite's brasses were made in England.

If possible, take off the brasses and examine them closely. If the screws resemble doughnuts, they are hand made and were made before 1800.

1630–1725

Brasses were small, sometimes engraved, simple in design.

1690–1730

Prior to 1730, edges were beveled and show marks of a file.

Designs were made by punches, gauged by the eye so that no two were exactly alike.

1702–49

Brass plate in shape of bat's wing with bail handles.

1730–80

Chippendale styles were engraved, larger, more ornate and heavier than those of the previous period. Also, rosettes with bail handles.

1780–1800

Escutcheons and knobs of enamel appeared. Sometimes sewing tables had ivory knobs. American furniture rarely had silver or silver-plated handles.

1780–1820

Hepplewhite period. Round or oval brass plates with bail handles shaped to fit the bottom curve; rectangles with cut corners. Both were fastened by threaded brass bolts, rather small in diameter whose nuts were either round, square or hexagonal. The shapes were stamped with relief designs of fruit, grain, eagles, temples, crocodiles, dogs, lions, serpents, deer, doves. Early country pieces sometimes had wrought-iron bail handles.

1790–1810

Sheraton period. Oblong, stamped brass plates with bails; circular flat knobs; rosette knobs. Designs same as Hepplewhite but more raised and ornate.

1820–30

Empire. Brass rosettes, larger (two inches) and flatter knobs; wooden mushroom or pressed glass knobs. Brass lion masks with ring hanging from nose.

1830 on

Early Victorian. Turned wood knobs of all kinds; fat teardrops of black lacquered wood hanging from elaborately stamped thin brass plates.

1850 on

Mid-Victorian. Machine-carved wooden handles in shape of leaves, nuts and fruits.

1885 on

As walnut became scarce, manufacturers learned how to handle oak, which was more plentiful and less expensive. This was the beginning of more commercial furniture. Handles were machine-stamped brass with thin bail handles.

1900 on

Same designs as previous period, but no longer solid brass. Brass color when polished turns to tin color. If in doubt, scratch back of plate.

Exceptions: Pieces of furniture made as late as 1825 often had brasses from the 1775–1800 period because cabinetmakers either had them in stock or reused old brasses.

CHAPTER 5

Bottoms

If everything else checks out, bottoms will tell you more. But if the piece is heavy, tall or near anything breakable, ask for permission and help when moving it.

How wide are the boards? The wider they are, the older the piece.

What kind of saw cut the wood? (See "Feel," Chapter 15.) Older pieces usually show shave marks left from hand tools. Because bottoms were left unsmooth or unfinished, the bottom is an ideal place to learn how the piece was made. (It's also the one place fakers forget to forge.)

Is there wear in the right places from sitting on the floor? If not, it may be the top of a two-section piece, a hanging cupboard or may be minus the original feet.

Is the bottom board dovetailed into the sides? This is an indication of a well-made piece of furniture and usually denotes age.

Are there screw marks or nail holes in any kind of pattern? This may indicate molding or feet were removed.

Are the feet original, or have they been replaced? Holes and lighter colored areas show where feet once stood. If the bottom shows such marking, what shape feet did it have?

If the piece now has Chippendale feet (see "Feet," Chapter 16), make sure there aren't holes at each corner where round Empire feet once stood. Since Empire feet were inserted directly through the bottom, the interior should also have holes at the corners. Empire pieces are often stripped of their veneer, dark finish and curves to make them look like early pine pieces. The bottom is often the only place that will reveal this backdating.

Conversely, if the piece now has Empire feet, but shows the markings of bracket or ogee feet from the Chippendale period, it may have been updated because of wear and be much older than you first guessed.

Last but not least: Are all the glue blocks in place? Glue blocks are triangular pieces of wood placed inside a piece where additional support is needed (i.e., inside ogee feet or at the waists of clocks, where the workman did not want to use nails). Are they all the same? Are they hand-carved? Run your finger over them to tell. Hand-carved glue blocks are another indication that the piece was made by a skilled craftsman and therefore more valuable.

See also: "Feel," "Feet," "Joining."

CHAPTER 6

Case Pieces, Chests

What started as a storage box or blanket chest with a lid grew into many other forms of six-board pieces. As drawers and feet were added and it became more high than long, chests, desks and highboys came into being.

During the 1600s, chests were used for storage. Turned vertically, they became cupboards used for display.

Pennsylvania chests were made from the early 1700s on. Large, low, sometimes with a drawer in the bottom, they often had painted decorations. As they became higher and narrower, they were called blanket chests.

With the advent of cabinetmaking, these chests became chests of drawers, highboys, lowboys and desks.

The high chest became very popular in Philadelphia, but never gained in popularity in England. The earliest high chests had flat tops.

During the Queen Anne period, the flat top remained popular, but the broken arch was introduced, sometimes flanked by finials. The shell decoration appears with pilasters sometimes flanking each side of the upper section.

Lowboys are usually composed of one to three drawers

on legs. A highboy is essentially a lowboy with a chest of drawers added to the top. Highboys can be dated in the following manner:

William and Mary feet	1680–1720	} flat tops
Queen Anne feet	1720–60	
Queen Anne feet with bonnet top	1720–60	
Ball and claw feet with bonnet or scroll top	1750–80	

A lowboy is usually of table height and is sometimes used as a dressing table.

Before 1750, case pieces were always dovetailed together. Sides were of a single piece of wood. As wide wood and time disappeared from 1800 on, paneled end pieces were introduced.

During the Chippendale period in England, the high chest had been replaced by a chest-on-chest and chest combined with an upper sectionlike cupboard sometimes called a linen press. Fine examples were made in New England.

During this period, dentil molding appeared at tops of cupboards and desks with fluted chamfered corners.

Good pieces of furniture (chests of drawers, desks, etc.) always have two layers of boards on top: the subtop, which is dovetailed to the bottom; and the top piece. The joining is then covered with molding. The only way to determine if the sides have been dovetailed to the top is to look inside the top corners.

On a highboy, it wasn't necessary to use two boards because the dovetail wouldn't show, but on desks, the dovetail in the top piece denotes quality.

The bottom half of a chest-on-chest is dovetailed, but not the top of the top half.

In cities, case pieces were made by many workers, each of whom had a different specialty. A signature, when found, could be that of one of the craftsmen and not necessarily that of the designer or shop owner. If a signature is found, check the *Directory of American Furniture Makers*.

The major innovations in case pieces were:

1690–1725

Puritan span. Chests with mushroom and inverted trumpet feet. Fronts with flat carving sometimes painted black, blue, red and green. Court cupboards (low cupboard on an open frame); press cupboards (lower section with doors or drawers, top with recessed doors).

1690–1725

William and Mary. Case pieces become more baroque, of larger proportions with teardrop pulls, curved stretchers, ball or bun feet with inverted cup or trumpet knees. Inlays, marquetry, scrolls and columns added. Highboys and lowboys appear on scene. Walnut with walnut and burl veneers.

1725–50

Queen Anne. Cabriole leg gains in popularity. Made of

solid woods in walnut, cherry, maple, mahogany, sunburst and shell carving; japanning.

1738–80

Newport block fronts used three-inch-thick wood in drawer fronts, although associated with Newport, Rhode Island, they were also made by Connecticut furniture makers.

1754–80

Chippendale. Secretary tops added to desks. Introduction of bamboo-type carving, fretwork, complicated foliate patterns, fluting, reeding, rococo, acanthus leaves. Elaborately carved aprons and skirts, bombé fronts. Ball and claw foot, bracket and ogee bracket. Gothic, Chinese and French influences.

1785–1810

Hepplewhite introduced tambour desks, china closets, sideboards. Less carving. Legs become square and tapered or made in French bracket. Designs of sunburst, conche shell, bellflower, eagle. Flat oval brasses, usually oval and sometimes round with designs of fruit, grain, eagles, temples, crocodiles, dogs, lions, serpents, deer, doves. Carvings of plumes, wheat, leaves, eagle, thunderbolt.

1790–1800

Glue used more extensively.

1790–1820

Sheraton. Mirrors were attached to dressers, legs turned. Fronts and sides were veneered in contrasting light and dark woods. Legs on chests are turned, reeded or ringed. Corner column supports extend through to legs. Carving of drapery festoons, wheat, thunderbolts, rosettes. Oblong brass pulls with bails, rosette knobs or lion head with hanging ring. Mahogany with satinwood, cherry with fancy maple.

1810–40

Empire. Large, bulky, heavy lines in cube and rectangular shapes. Radical change of style with downward sloping curves, paneled sides, concave curved front legs, columns at sides, winged legs and animal feet. Bold carving, much veneer, ogee molding, cyma curves. Projecting round brass knobs stamped with eagle, George Washington or patriotic motif; ring pull hanging from brass lion head. Round ball feet extend through bottom corners.

1840 on

Gothic arch with trefoil, cusp finials, crotchet carvings.

1840–80

Spool turnings.

1860–80

Painted cottage pieces.

1868–1900

Wardrobes and bookcases. Furniture produced in sets rather than individual pieces. Victorian designs in oak, poplar, walnut, elm, birch and ash. Applied carvings.

See also: "Desks," "Doors," "Drawers," "Feet," "Finish," "Brasses," "Joining," "Moldings," "Nails," "Styles."

CHAPTER 7

Casters

Casters or rollers were wheel devices added to make furniture mobile. Casters were used on lighter pieces while rollers were made for heavier furniture. Although casters are not an indication of age, they may add another clue to the age of the piece.

Early 1700s

Leather casters were used on English furniture.

Late 1700s

Casters had brass sockets with iron or brass rollers. The sockets were square, round, hexagonal and octagonal and fit on the outside of the foot. Called cup casters, they are rare, and were added to tables from 1800 on.

1790

Sheraton put iron casters on beds to ease movement.

1810

Duncan Phyfe designed delicate brass casters, which were manufactured in England. He also originated the brass paw foot which held its own caster.

1810 on

Machine-made brass casters appeared, designed to fit *inside* the leg.

1820 on

Empire tables with large wooden paw feet containing their own casters made of metal.

1840 on

Two innovations made the scene: porcelain casters and casters with bearings to facilitate movement in any direction.

Exceptions: Old casters may be added to new pieces. Old pieces which originally did not have casters (i.e., banquet tables, chairs) often have casters added to raise their height.

Furniture which once had casters will retain markings on outer leg or have holes in the bottom of the foot.

If a piece is missing one or all of its original casters, a restorer will usually add reproductions. These look exactly like the originals, but are machine made and smooth to the touch.

CHAPTER 8
Chairs

Chairs will teach you more about styles and periods than any other kind of furniture. You can visualize what period room goes with a chair. Not only that, they are comfortable to sit in while studying them.

Sit in a chair to see if it's worn where your hands rest and where you hook your feet on the rung.

If the chair is a slat-back or ladder back, look at where your shoulders rest against the back. Are the original score marks worn off the posts from age?

How high is the seat? Older chairs were made for shorter people and were also worn down through the years and from resting on dirt floors. If the chair seat is of modern height, examine the bottoms of the legs to see if additions have been made. Feel the bottom of the legs (see "Feet"). Run your hand over the bottom of the seat to feel for roughness (see "Bottoms") and saw marks. If it's smooth, it may not be old. Look at the bottom for signature or initials of the maker.

Are the legs and posts round? With age, older pieces don't remain round, but shrink through the width of the grain, becoming oval in circumference. Measure the round section with calipers. If perfectly round, it's not old. Minor shrinkage occurs across the grain in square legs also.

Get out of the chair and check the back of the finials or posts. The two outer sides of finials should be more worn than the inner edges (from resting against the wall). Check the width of the stretcher across the front legs for wear. On old chairs, it can be worn through as much as 50 per cent. If a chair has two front rungs, the bottom one should be the most worn or that rung which is most easy to hook your heel on.

Front legs of early chairs are rarely perfectly flat because they were dragged across the floor by the backs, with the weight resting on the front legs.

Study regional pieces before trying to master periods.

The earliest American chairs were primitive slab seat stools. The legs often stood at an outward angle, instead of straight to give it more stability. The earliest chairs copied this splay or cant leg for the same reason. These early stools grew out at the side to become benches and later grew up to become tables and chairs.

Slat-back Chair (made in all periods)

Flat ladder-back pieces fitted (mortised into back posts) rather than curved like ladder backs. The arms were socketed into the posts like a light bulb. Early slat backs had as many as seven in number. Later slat backs had fewer slats and the turning on the legs was less pronounced. Country slat backs were hand whittled with a drawing knife. Made in native woods (hickory, ash, maple).

In the 1600s, there were few chairs. The few they had were usually reserved for the master or the important guest. Others sat on chests, benches or stools.

1650–90

Puritan. Wainscot chair, back and seat solid panels, flat carving, turned legs with straight stretchers. The Carver had turned spindles in back, with a rush seat. The Brewster had two rows of vertical-turned spindles with additional spindles under arms and seat.

1690–1725

William and Mary. Stiff elegant chairs. The Cane Chair had a tall back with caning on the back and seat. Sometimes found today with upholstery in place of the caning. The Banister Chair resembled a stair railing with carved crest top, turned legs and downward molded arms. Those made with red or black leather seats were called Boston chairs.

Transitional: round seat, spoon feet, banister back.

1725–50

Queen Anne. Light graceful curves, often with shell at center back, sometimes center seat skirt. Stiles often curved. Center splat-shaped vase or violin. Seat horseshoe or compass shape. Front legs cabriole, rear plain, round or stump. Curve of back sometimes fits human shape vertically.

Transitional: Queen Anne chair with ball and claw foot.

Windsor Chair (also called the stick chair) 1725–1825

It's usually a good yardstick to say that the more spindles on the back of a Windsor, the rarer the chair. Some experts consider nine spindles the ideal.

Windsors, known for their bold turnings, remained light in feeling until 1825. Their seats were shaped to fit human bottoms and were balanced in proportion.

There are distinct differences in better Windsors. In seats, the higher the center ridge, the better the chair.

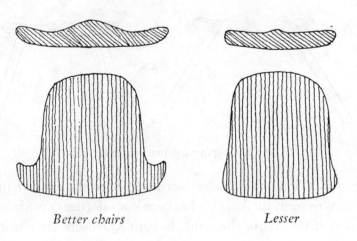

Better chairs   *Lesser*

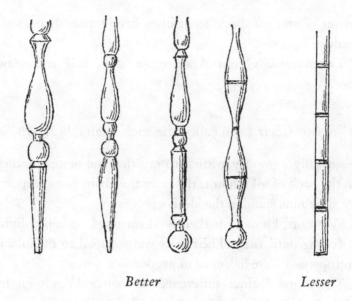

Better   *Lesser*

Legs with ball turnings, rounds, rings and half rounds are preferable to the bamboo.

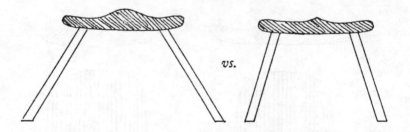

vs.

And a bold splay leg marks a finer chair.

On Windsors, it is also best to examine the ends of the arms to see if the knuckle has been cut off (the curved section at the end of the arm). English Windsors are usually made of oak and are heavier in appearance and weight than American chairs.

On American chairs, the backs and spindles were usually made of hickory with seats of pine or maple. For this reason, they were painted green, red or black.

Back spindles stuck into the seat as well as the legs. Because of age shrinkage, vertical pieces may have risen above horizontal sections (i.e., sticking through the back bow).

The earliest Windsor was the early low back.

The comb back was an extension on top of the loop in the shape of a comb. This is the most esteemed of Windsors. Variations include the fan back and the sack back. More sophisticated versions had more delicately turned ears (the top corners on the back).

The loop back, also called the bow or balloon back, was so named because the spindles were framed by a single piece of wood bent into a loop.

The Windsors mentioned above were made between 1725 and 1825. In the latter 1800s, the later low back was lower and usually rose a little over a foot from the seat. It came into popularity in the Victorian period and is now often called a firehouse or barroom Windsor. If the seat is made of a single plank, it was made prior to 1840.

The brace-back Windsor: two sticks of wood in the shape of a V rising from seat to the top of the back. This form is as rare as the writing arm and the staggered spindle.

On country pieces, the stretchers were spoke shaved, while city pieces have turned stretchers.

The arrow back of the 1820s is a variation of the Windsor.

Pennsylvania Windsors had a ball foot, while New England Windsors (considered the most delicate) flowed into a gentle taper below the vase or straight cone.

1754–80

Chippendale. Proportions much as Queen Anne but different in line. Slats pierced, curved and swagged. Backs more intricate with top rail curved into cupid's bow. Splat pierced. Rails and stiles often carved in intricate foliate designs. Later Chippendale side rails not tenoned through back legs (1800). Slip seats often replaced with padded seat with stuffing over the rails. Hard-pine blocks denote Philadelphia or southern origin. Mahogany slat back made from 1780 to 1800.

Wing back. Prior to 1788, the wings of wing chairs started at the seat rail with the arm attached to the wing. After this date, to facilitate the curve of the Federal style, makers built the arm into the back, then added the wing. Upholstery on pieces usually follows the lines of the frame. If not, the frame can be felt through the upholstery.

1800–10

Transitional Chippendale had ladder-back design.

1786–1810

Hepplewhite. Shield, oval back. Square seat shape curves at four sides, smoother curves throughout. More vertical designs replacing later horizontal ladder-back Chippendale. Urn and feather designs, garlands of flowers, shields, urns, vase.

1805

Arms of armchairs curve upward to meet corners at back.

1805–15

Bell-shaped seats (mostly New York and Philadelphia).

1790–1815

Sheraton. Rectangular back with carved tassels, rosettes; serpentine front on seat, curved seat. Oval back is more English than American. Turned legs.

1794–1846

Duncan Phyfe. Grecian influence. Chairs look like ballet dancers. Thick top rail and stiles joined in one piece with seat rail. Ogee scroll back, cross or lattice back, lyre or harp. Carving on top rail thunderbolt, sheaf of wheat and drapery festoon. Splat lyre and harp. Grecian front and back legs. Mahogany.

1815–40

Empire. Strangely enough, chairs in this period do not follow the heavy massive proportions of the other pieces. Many were nicely painted and conformed to styles of earlier periods. Graceful curves, sometimes point at top center back. Solid vase-shape chair splat, simple graceful legs and feet.

1818–29

The first Hitchcock chairs were made with rush seats. Later styles had cane or solid wood seats. During this period, his chairs were signed with a stencil reading "L. Hitchcock, Hitchcocksville, Connecticut, Warranted."

1829–43

In 1826, Hitchcock built a larger factory which ran into financial difficulties in 1829. At this time, he took on a partner named Arba Alford. During this period, chairs were labeled "Hitchcock, Alford & Co., Warranted."

1843–52

Hitchcock started a new business in Unionville and began marking his chairs "Lambert Hitchcock, Unionville, Connecticut." His partner began making chairs with his brother Alfred and signed them "Alford & Company." Chairs made today in Hitchcocksville (now Riverton) use the first factory stencil with the "N" reversed. To differentiate between today's chair and the original, "H.C.Co." is added under the front of the seat.

1840–75

Victorian. Comfort and usefulness dominate. Countless types and styles flowed from the makers, ranging from light side chairs to fluffy upholstered armchairs. The Morris chair was invented. From 1850–70 some of the most sought-after chairs of today came into being. They had finger carving, carved frames and varied cabriole legs.

Advances in power and machines enabled makers to produce chairs in sets of six and eight. Other sets included the parlor set, the gentleman's upholstered armchair and the companion lady chair. Some of the numerous chairs produced during this period were:

Writing armchair	Balloon-back side chair
Morris chair	Captain's chair
Spindle-back side chair	Slat-back Windsor
Kitchen U-back Windsor (oak)	Spindle-back dining-room Windsor
Rocking chair (copy Boston rocker)	Platform rocker
	Cane-back rocker
Desk armchair	Bar-back side chair
Gothic armchair	Gothic hall chair
Sleepy Hollow armchair	Oval-back armchair
Balloon-back armchair	Balloon-back lady's chair

CHAPTER 9

Clocks

Few clocks were made in the United States before 1750. Prior to the Revolutionary War, there were only sixty-seven clockmakers in the colonies. Before 1800, the average household had only sundials, noon marks, hourglasses, turnip-sized, triple-cased silver watches and an uncanny knack for telling time by the sun.

During the Revolutionary War, when there was a shortage of materials and workmen, some works were fabricated of wood. Brass faces on tall clocks are usually pre-Revolutionary War, while painted faces are post-Revolutionary War.

In 1809, the first of the famous Connecticut clock partnerships was founded with Eli Terry, Seth Thomas and Silas Hoadley composing the firm. Terry's pillar and scroll clock was widely copied in the Connecticut Valley. A few years later, in 1825, Chauncey Jerome, in partnership with his brother Noble and Elijah Darrow, introduced a patented bronze looking-glass clock. Twelve years later, he invented the stamped brass movement which revolutionized clockmaking in America. By the time of the Civil War, the number of clockmakers in the United States had climbed to eight hundred and fifty.

The name on the face of a clock is usually that of the works maker, not the casemaker. On Eli Terry clocks, for instance, the patent on the works was sold for $.25. The eight or nine makers of the Eli Terry clock usually pasted their own printed label on the back of the works facing the back door.

If a clock has a name, check reference books at the library to locate more information. To determine the age of the clock, add twenty years to the maker's birth to find out the earliest date he could have made the clock. If the maker was born in 1780, he started making clocks in

1800, therefore you know that your clock is post-1800.

The clock's movement and case were always made by different people. Casemakers couldn't sign the clock, but they could sign the case. There are more unnamed clocks than named because the works were traded to casemakers in return for making cases. A clock apprentice couldn't sign clocks during his apprenticeship or if he didn't complete his training.

Sometimes clock works have a date inscribed on the back. Some authentic American works were dated by the maker on the back of the movement itself. Most early American makers bought works from England and commissioned a local cabinetmaker to build a case around it.

Look carefully at the clock. Is it an old case? Does the case look like it goes with the works or have they been married (matched at a later date)? How do the works fit into the case? Is the wood border or frame around the face the same proportion as the frame in the door? When the door is closed, does the inside border show in different areas than it should?

On grandfather clocks, if you can take off the hood, are the works screwed into the support bridge through the same holes, or are there holes where screws once were that don't match the screw holes in the mounting board?

Open the bottom door. Do the weights hang in the center of the depth? (They should not hang toward the front.) If these don't check out, the chances are the works and case are more of a divorce than a marriage.

Smell inside the clock. If it's old, it should remind you of an attic on a rainy day.

1700–1850

Grandfather (or tall) clock. Earliest had flat top and heavy cornice, square dial.

1725 on

Arch top on case and dial.

1750 on

Scroll or broken-arch top with Chippendale-style fretwork.

1760–1810

Moon face, days of week, month.

Late 1700s

Grandmother clocks, four feet (more or less) tall.

1780–1820

Wooden works.

1800 on

Wall clocks.

1802

Banjo, gilt frame, finial above round dial, brass brackets along center panel, painted decoration on center panel, glass panel in bottom section.

1815–40

Pillar and scroll clock.

1820

Mantel and shelf clocks. Although all mantels are shelf clocks, the reverse is not true. The mantel was more elegant. After spring power, mantel clocks went to every form, description and size possible.

1840–50

Steeple clock, rectangular mantel case with painted panel below dial, tiny turrets or steeple on top.

1840

Fancy shapes, hourglass, acorn, lyre, cast iron, bronze, marble, papier-mâché, exotic woods.

1800–40

Shelf clocks: some spring driven, most weight driven. These were made in eight-day and thirty-hour mechanisms. If the hole for winding is below the 4 and 8, it is an eight-day clock. If the hole is above the 4 and 8, it is the less expensive thirty-hour clock. All early mantel clocks (i.e., pillar and scroll) were weight driven.

Reverse Painting on Glass in Clocks

There is no sure way to determine if glass is original in the door of a clock. However, the style of picture and ornamentation had definite time periods.

Up to 1825

All glass was painted by hand.

1833–35

Gold-leaf borders began to decline in size. Houses took up less of picture. More trees and bushes appeared in scene to save time in painting. (Manufacturers paid about $.01½ to paint a glass.)

1840–50

Etched and frosted transfers made with varnish and sugar appeared. Can be identified by fine lines and subtle shadings not obtainable in hand painting.

1840–60

Whole glass was stenciled.

1844–48

Stopped painting buildings completely and switched to geometric designs. Top and bottom glasses often did not match in color or design.

1845

Empire column or cornice clocks appeared.

1850

Decals appeared and were gradually combined over transfers.

See also: "Backs," "Bottoms," "Doors," "Fakes," "Feel," "Hinges," "Interior," "Labels," "Screws."

CHAPTER 10

Desks

Desks were originally large wooden boxes made to hold writing materials or Bibles. Some were flat. Others had slant tops. (See also: "Feet," "Legs," "Brasses," "Hinges.")

1650–1700

Boxes as described above.

1680–1710

Boxes were attached to a topless frame on legs instead of being set on a table.

1700–50

As the frame grew into drawers, the slant-top desk was born. Although it had more drawers, one third of its height remained in legs. Many that looked simple on the outside had elaborately crafted interiors.

1740–80

The desk bottom became three to four drawers in a base set

on feet rather than legs, with a desk top. The writing section developed variations: the fall front (drawer front was hinged), pull-out writing shelf and the quarter cylinder front.

When a bookcase was added to the top of the desk, it became known as a secretary. As this development became fancier, doors were added with arched tops. Earlier secretaries had paneled doors (see "Doors," Chapter 12).

1750

The kneehole desk came into being, with three to four full drawers in the base with a desk top. (To determine the age of a kneehole desk, see "Styles.")

1760 on

Miller or bookkeeper's desk. Top slant-lid desk on high tapered or squared-off legs. Used while standing up or seated on high stool. Store desk is similar but without legs. Usually set on counter, it is slightly smaller in size.

1780–1800

Hepplewhite replaced the ball and claw foot with out-curved French bracket foot. He also originated the tambour desk with a flat folding leaf. Strips of wood were glued onto a piece of canvas, making a flexible sheet that operated vertically like a roll-top desk or horizontally like doors. Hepplewhite often substituted tall legs for the drawers in the base. This is called a desk-on-frame.

1785–90

By the Hepplewhite and Sheraton periods, small glass panes appeared in the doors. These small panes grew larger over the years as glass became more plentiful. The larger the glass, the later the piece (see "Doors").

1800–70

Schoolmaster's desk. Early styles have square tapered legs; middle, turned; later, spool.

1820 on

Butler's desk. Exterior looks like bureau. Drawer front drops down to form writing surface.

1820–40

Empire desk. Heavy legs, pillars, cyma curves, heavy woods and veneers. What appears as an Empire desk is often a square piano without its musical parts.

1837–50

Early Victorian. Same designs as Empire but more ornamentation with spool turned legs (see "Legs").

1840 on

Partner's desk, also called accounting desk, made for two people to use simultaneously. Can be of seated or standing height.

1850–65

Louis XV influence, a combination of Empire curves and Victorian carving, oval panels, custom made of mahogany and rosewood.

1850–75

Mid-Victorian. Flat-top library or writing tables, usually with leather liner on top. Sometimes top has been added with various arrangements of doors, drawers, places for account books, etc. Gothic details (i.e., quatre foil and arches), carved fruit or leaf designs, burl veneers, softwood stained to resemble mahogany. Movable shelves, round wooden knobs, brass pendant with ring handle. Earlier desks in this period were of mahogany; later, of black walnut.

1865–80

Secretary table-type base with cupboards on either side of top, joined by rail and topped with crestlike moldings.

1874–80

Wooten's patent desk, called an office in itself. A combination of everything in a single frame. Cylinder front top, heavily paneled.

1875–1901

Late Victorian. Oak. Slant-top desk over shelves. Sometimes had mirror and side shelves over top section.

44

CHAPTER 11

Dimensions

Earlier pieces were often one of a kind, made to the specifications of the buyer, the design of the maker or to fit the architectural style and proportion of a house.

Very often the architect or designer of the house also designed and made the furniture (Robert Adams, Samuel McIntyre and Thomas Jefferson, for instance).

While George Washington did have some furniture brought over from England, a large amount was made by his slaves under the direction of his master cabinetmakers. This is an example of how sizes gained their proportions. Later, as cabinetmakers moved into business establishments (Chippendale, Hepplewhite, Sheraton, Phyfe, etc.) they not only built to personal specifications, but made pieces for stock and inventory purposes. This was the beginning of standard measurements (heights, widths, etc.).

There are certain yardsticks that would indicate what something is by its measurements.

Lowboys are one fifth smaller than highboy bases. If a top has been added to a lowboy at a later date, it will make the piece look top heavy.

Eating tables measure twenty-eight inches to thirty inches in height, shorter than modern furniture.

The standard height for chair seats was approximately seventeen to eighteen inches. However, due to shorter ancestors, it is not unusual to find a set of chairs in varying heights because the legs were cut off to conform to the individual.

Butterfly tables usually measure from twenty-five to twenty-seven inches high. Anything higher would indicate a reproduction.

Desks: The writing area or lid is approximately thirty inches high from the floor. Secretary tops should be half as deep as the lower section.

CHAPTER 12

Doors

Flush

Doors on early primitive furniture were made of a single piece of wood or boards joined together with a cross or diagonal brace, much like a barn door. These doors were usually set flush with the outside edge of the piece.

46

DOORS

Paneled

As craftsmen improved their methods during the mid-1700s, they began to set panels into doors, much as glass fits in a picture frame. To break the monotony of the straight line, workmen sometimes carved scallops or curves on the inner edge of the frame. Two-section pieces usually had wood-paneled doors top and bottom.

Glass

Before long, furniture makers realized that glass was not only cheaper but less time-consuming to use than wood. Buyers preferred glass because they could display their prized possessions inside the doors without worrying about the collection of dust.

The earliest glass in doors was called bull's-eye. Round, thick, with a swirl that meets in the center, it is rare. To test whether a bull's-eye is old, feel the back. It should have a rough spot from the pontil mark, much like the bottom of an old bottle.

1785–1840

During the Hepplewhite period (about 1785), glass became available in flat sheets with a slightly wavy appearance. Sometimes tiny bubbles appeared in the surface. The first glass panes were small, but as years passed, they became larger. If a piece has been well cared for, it should have at least one of its original panes. Conversely, if it ap-

47

pears to have *all* of the original panes, it would be a near miracle. The chances are the panes are replacements from old windowpanes. If this is the case, examine all other parts closely.

1840–1900

Glass changed little in appearance until the mid-Victorian period (1840) when it became smooth and clear. By this time, door frames often contained a single sheet of glass. By the late Victorian period (1890–1900), display cases were being made with curved glass in the side and top sections.

Wear

Examine a door for wear and evidence of lock or knob replacements. Some doors never had knobs because they were used to safeguard valuables instead of storing everyday utensils. In such cases, you will often find a later knob and signs of a missing lock.

Open the door to see where your hand rests when holding it open. Is it worn there? If not, find out where the worn spot is. If it is at the bottom of the door, it may be the top half of a two-section piece. The bottom half (if that's what it is) should be worn on the inside top edge where the hand rests while holding the door open.

Some doors were made with rotating wooden latches which left a worn mark in the shape of a half-moon where the latch swung over the door. The deeper the mark, the older the piece. On very old cupboard doors that were used frequently, the latch often wore completely through the wood jamb, requiring the latch to be moved an inch higher or lower.

If the wooden latch was later updated with a metal or wooden knob, this half-moon indentation will remain, indicating the piece is earlier than the hardware.

Larger doors, because of their weight, often required strap hinges. Although the hinges were strong, the pins on which they swung usually wore through with age, causing the door to sag and rub against the frame. Check the bottom of the door for evidence of wear from rubbing. If you find these worn spots, but the hinges now seem to be working properly, check where the hinges fit into the frame. Early hinges were mortised in place with chisels which left gouge marks. If the hinges do not fit exactly, the chances are they have been replaced. If this is true, they cannot be used as a measuring stick for determining the age of the piece.

If you are fairly sure they *are* the original hinges, turn to Chapter 18 ("Hinges," of course) and read on.

CHAPTER 13

Drawers

Drawers can be the most eloquent parts of an antique and one of the first places you should check.

Pull out a drawer. See how it is made as well as where it is worn.

Are all the drawers the same color and workmanship? Check to see if any have been replaced or repaired. Were the drawers made for this particular frame? Run your hand under the bottom of a drawer and inside the top of the piece to see if they feel the same.

Try putting the drawer in upside down. In old, well-made pieces, it will usually slide in both ways.

Are the runners worn? Runners are the strips of wood along each side of the bottom. Have they been replaced? If so, is the bottom of the drawer also worn? As drawer supports wore down, they were usually turned over. If they have been worn down, turned over and then replaced with new runners, it is usually an indication of a very old piece.

Are the drawers worn in the right places? This is usually at the front corners and drawers closest to waist height.

DRAWERS

Top drawers were used more than bottom ones. If the piece has small drawers, the next larger one is usually the most worn.

Are the corners of the drawers dovetailed? Dovetailing is a method of cutting wedges along the edges of two pieces which are then joined. When placed together, they interlock, preventing separation. Early dovetails had to fit snug because glue had not been invented.

If the drawer is dovetailed, how wide are the dovetails? Larger dovetails were used in older pieces. Before 1750, craftsmen often made only one dovetail in a drawer joint, and never more than two. Handmade dovetails (before 1880) are not as even as those made by machine. Look for scribe marks (pencil lines made by a ruler showing where dovetails were to be cut). Machine dovetails are closer together, evenly spaced and precise in fit. Drawers made by finer craftsmen had dovetails at both front and rear corners.

1700–1800

Dovetails handcrafted. Refinement depended on individual craftsman.

1748–80

Drawer fronts of block front pieces made in Newport were carved out of wood at least three inches thick, with one long dovetail twice as long as the others. Block front pieces are extremely rare.

1760–1800

As their ability increased, craftsmen became more competitive, trying to see how long or how intricate they could make a dovetail. Size depended on the size of the piece, but some were as long as three inches. The more refined the workmanship, the closer to the 1800s.

1800 on

Dovetails at both front and back corners, glued in place.

1800 on

Machine dovetails of various patents and designs, very evenly spaced, no scribe or saw marks.

What kind of secondary wood is used in drawer sides and bottom? (See "Woods," Chapter 39.) American pieces usually have chestnut, poplar or pine as a secondary wood, whereas English makers used oak.

The secondary wood in drawers often tells where the piece was made. For instance, Virginia pieces were made with pine as a secondary wood because of the abundance of yellow pine in the Appalachian Mountains, whereas Maryland makers used poplar. A walnut chest with pine secondary wood is more apt to be Virginian than Maryland.

If a chest of drawers has a big deep drawer in the bottom, it is usually the bottom part of a chest-on-chest.

CHAPTER 14

Fakes

If an antique has one or more parts that do not seem right or do not fall into the same time period as the rest of the piece, check it over carefully to make sure it is not a fake or a reproduction. If you discover it is not a period piece but like it and want it, point out these discrepancies to the seller, and the chances are you can buy it for a fraction of the original price.

No matter how well a fake is done, there will be at least one flaw. For instance, two gun experts decided to "make" a rare gun and sell it to a nationally renowned gun authority in order to test his expertise. They completely built a new "antique" around the stock of an old gun, burying it in a combination of earth and cellar mold to duplicate the smell. That worked. The one thing they couldn't duplicate was the taste of old metal (a chemical reaction that hits your tongue when an old gun is licked). Despite this flaw, they succeeded in selling the gun to the expert, proving they knew something that he didn't.

Phony labels: At the turn of the nineteenth century, there were approximately one thousand cabinetmakers in

New York City alone, but only two signed their work. Few antiques carried a label (see "Labels," Chapter 21).

If old wood has been used to make a new piece (i.e., barn doors and siding), the ends of the boards will show circular saw marks.

Although the edges of a piece have been dulled to suggest wear on the outside, it is impossible to duplicate the gray patina of age inside. Make sure it has a mellow color throughout the interior.

Run your hand over the underside of the top and under bottoms of drawers to make sure the piece is rough, hand planed and dressed. If it is smooth, examine other sections.

If any plywood has been used on drawers or backs, watch out. Plywood wasn't invented until 1900.

Check the bottom ends of boards for signs of paint colors, an indication the piece was made from some other wood.

Check saw cuts across the grain. If old lumber was used to make new antiques, or bigger pieces have been cut down and rearranged, the saw cuts will be smooth. It is difficult to imitate old saw marks in cut or stain.

Check the thickness of the boards. Modern boards are not a full inch, but are cut one-eighth inch less than a full inch. Check width of boards. Modern boards seldom run wider than six to eight inches and must be glued together.

Make sure the underside of the drawers feels the same as the underside of the top. New pieces are often built around old drawers.

If the piece is made of pine, check the size of the knotholes. Old pine did not have large knots. If a piece had any knots, they were very small and seldom more than one or two.

Oxalic acid is used to make poplar look like pine. The only way to tell if this has been done is by the grain. Poplar has green and yellow streaks. Often a board is half light and half dark. No matter what color it has been stained, these markings will show through.

Wormholes: If made naturally in furniture, they show as tiny dots. If the wood has been cut from something else, wormholes will often appear as channels.

Nails: One dealer who made "new" antiques from old wood in the old manner couldn't duplicate one thing: old nails. So he used nippers on the head of the nail to square it, and then hit it with a torch to turn it black and give it an early old iron color (see "Nails," Chapter 26).

Look for filled nail holes on parts where no nails would have been (indication it was made from something else).

If you see countersunk nails or puttied holes anywhere on a piece, find out why, especially if they are round. Old nails were square or rectangular and if the piece is old, the puttied holes should be square or rectangular. Round holes would indicate modern nails or screws are under the putty. This can mean a piece has been cut down from something else, or the hole is hiding a repair. Examine the other side and see where the screws or nails go, and why.

Fakers sometimes bury wooden and metal pieces in the ground or manure pile, or stain them with tea and coffee, or put case pieces in smokehouses to darken the wood.

Smoke-darkened pieces will smell like a fire sale and smudge easily. Fakers also cover pieces with lye and mud for instant aging.

Spoke-shaved planks are not an indication of age. Manufacturers of furniture used them during the Empire period. On fine pieces like tables, spoke shave marks were never left in the finished product. They were always taken out with a smoothing plane. If the spoke shave marks are too obvious, beware.

Some fakers strip Victorian gingerbread from dressers to imitate early pine pieces, or change the feet and hardware on Empire pieces to make them appear as early country or Chippendale.

Beware of very early pieces that have been glued. Glue was not invented until 1750 and did not come into regular use until 1780.

Watch out if the bracket or butterfly leaf on a table is scalloped. They weren't originally made that way.

If a desk lid has supports that extend and retract automatically, it is a reproduction. Period desks were not automatic.

When a molding is missing on the top of a piece and has to be added, it is often not the same wood or the same age as the rest of the piece. To offset this without going to a great deal of trouble, some fakers rub stove black into the wood, and then after it dries, add basement dirt. If you are aware of this, it is obvious. Dust doesn't fall up, and smoke from a fireplace darkens very gradually toward the top. If you want to make sure it is age, test with your thumbnail.

There are many ways of aging a piece. Screws and nails

are beaten into the top. Other pieces are beaten with chains. Edges are rasped in appropriate places. Look for marks where they wouldn't normally grow with wear.

Other fakers pour burning shellac on top or submit a piece to ammonia vapors. This will age wood fifty years overnight.

Remember, no matter how well a fake is done, there will be at least one flaw.

CHAPTER 15

Feel

Never buy anything you don't touch and feel. Oftentimes your hand can detect what your eyes do not see. True wear cannot be reproduced.

Run your hand slowly over a table top to see if the boards were hand planed. As your hand slides across the grain, the wood will feel almost alive to your touch. If it was hand planed, you will actually feel a slight rise in certain areas.

Pull out a drawer and run your hand over its bottom. Old planes had blades with slightly curved edges that left ripply marks.

Are the edges worn? The edges should be soft, not hard like new furniture, and have slight indentations from wear.

Feel the bottom of the feet, the corners of drawer fronts, the edges of doors where they were opened or held open.

If a piece has been sanded too smooth and given hard edges on the outside, but you think it is old, feel inside the drawer fronts and bottoms of feet for wear.

Run your hand over the inside of the piece to find mending that does not show on the outside. Oftentimes, repairs are so skillfully made the only way to detect them is by touch. Feel the underside of a table top or case piece to make sure it feels the same as the drawers. Sometimes new furniture is built out of old wood around old drawers.

On the interior, does your hand detect small ridges of glue that were not removed after a repair? If so, examine the piece carefully to see why the repair was made.

In a solid end piece, feel inside and out for cracks. Sometimes sides of paneled end pieces have been replaced with solid wood ends to make them look older. If the wood has started cracking, it may be evidence of this, and could cause the whole side to fall out at a later date. Feel the inside to make sure the side feels the same as the back and front.

Run your hand over the legs. In early days, sandpaper was unknown. Old turning lathes ran slowly, leaving shallow spiral grooves running around the leg which can be felt by hand or seen with a magnifying glass.

Feel inside drawer fronts to see if the hardware has been replaced (see Chapter 4, "Brasses").

See also: "Backs," "Brasses," "Bottoms," "Drawers," "Joining," "Periods."

CHAPTER 16

Feet

The earliest American pieces had chunky fat feet because they rested on dirt floors. These feet were ball shaped. If flattened, the foot was called a bun, melon or onion ball.

On small chairs, the front of the feet are usually worn and more rounded than the back feet from dragging them across the room. Sometimes the back of the rear legs is worn from tipping back against the wall.

The exact part of the foot that comes in contact with the floor will be darker than the rest, finely polished from wear and almost black in color. Run your hand over the bottom of the foot. The black area will feel smooth, while the surrounding area will feel rough where dotage (rot from age) has set in.

The American ball and claw foot was larger than the English. The Philadelphia foot was more squat and held the ball firmly in the claw. The New England ball and claw had one talon resting on the ball, while the New York foot had a square ball with the claw following the same shape. Massachusetts had a hairy claw and Newport makers made a loose claw with a tendon over an oval ball.

Although ball and claw and ball and talon are used interchangeably, there is a difference in semantics. The claw shape is thicker and refers to an animal, while a talon is more delicate and refers to the bird species.

Ball feet on Empire pieces, if original, went all the way through the bottom of chests and cupboards. If they have been removed, there is usually a hole left at the corners. If ball feet have been added at a later date, they usually do not go through the piece but are attached from the bottom. If the piece has Chippendale-style feet but has holes at the corners, chances are it is an Empire piece reconstructed to look older.

You will often find that feet have been replaced because of breakage or rot. Unfortunately, because of fashion or bad taste they are sometimes replaced with feet from the wrong period. If examination shows that this is the case, a sum of the other parts will clearly spell out what type feet the piece should have.

If the feet do not match the period of the piece, examine all other parts carefully to see if there have been other replacements. If a chair checks out on all points but has flat feet that do not show signs of wear, it may be because someone (in an effort to make the chair more presentable) sawed off the bottoms to make them even. If this is true, it will have a hard edge on the bottom of the legs but be worn elsewhere.

Puritan (1650–90)

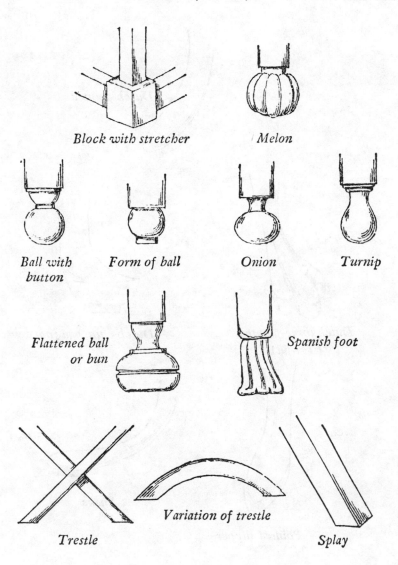

Block with stretcher

Melon

Ball with button

Form of ball

Onion

Turnip

Flattened ball or bun

Spanish foot

Trestle

Variation of trestle

Splay

61

Queen Anne (1725–50)

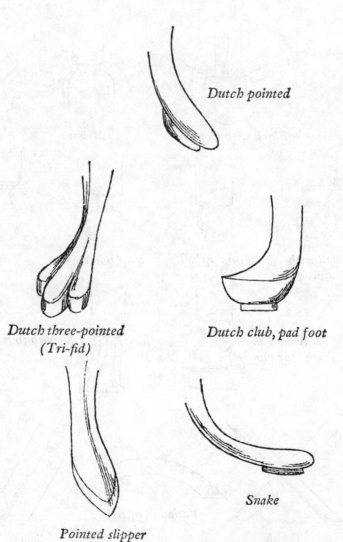

Dutch pointed

Dutch three-pointed
(Tri-fid)

Dutch club, pad foot

Pointed slipper

Snake

Chippendale (1754–80)

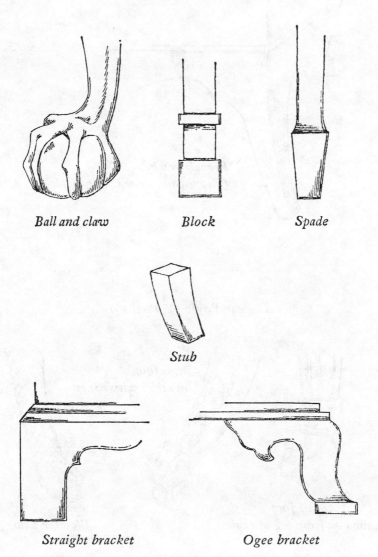

Ball and claw   Block   Spade

Stub

Straight bracket   Ogee bracket

Hepplewhite (1785–1810)

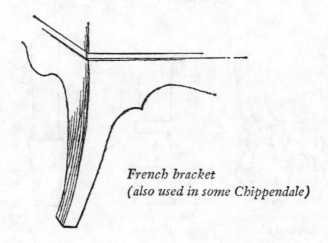

French bracket
(also used in some Chippendale)

Duncan Phyfe (1794–1846)

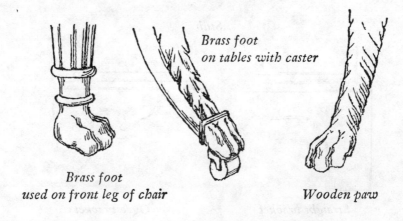

Brass foot
on tables with caster

Brass foot
used on front leg of chair

Wooden paw

Sheraton (1790–1810)

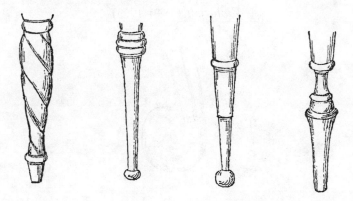

Variations of turned feet

Empire (1815–40)

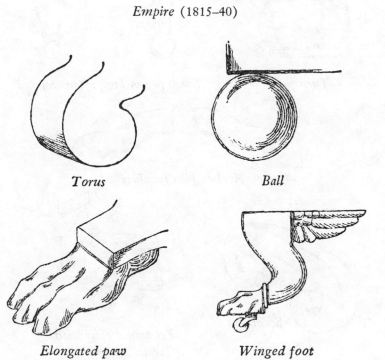

Torus

Ball

Elongated paw

Winged foot

Victorian (1840–1900)

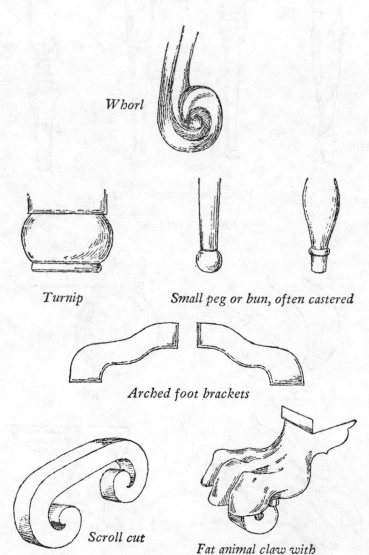

Whorl

Turnip

Small peg or bun, often castered

Arched foot brackets

Scroll cut

Fat animal claw with caster underneath

CHAPTER 17

Finish

If the wood shows through the finish in worn spots and no other colors can be seen, the finish is usually original.

Other indications are signs of everyday use like burn marks from candles. Or, for instance, a heavy piece of furniture (like a corner cupboard) that stood in the same room as a fireplace over a period of years would grow gradually darker toward the top. The finish should be worn where used every day.

The earliest finish was shellac. In the 1800s, a varnish stain was invented to cover inferior woods like poplar. Shellac, varnish and lacquer have changed little over the years. The important thing in analyzing the finish is to know which of the three it is so that you don't injure it while cleaning the piece.

Shellac separates into little circles, darker than the finish. Varnish checks into squares, and lacquer separates into rectangles. Each is applied with a different kind of binder. Shellac is bound with alcohol, varnish with turpentine, and lacquer with lacquer thinner. When cleaning a piece, it is important that you not use the original binder or you will dissolve the original finish.

Often a piece has several coats of paint that must be removed in order to find the original finish. So that you don't run these layers of paint together, or into the first layer, it is best to remove them by scraping. Old paint flakes and chips easily because it has dried out (see "Paint," Chapter 27). Do not use paint remover. It will dissolve the paint and mix it into the subsurfaces, harming the original finish.

Early furniture makers often used several different kinds of wood for strength and then painted the piece to disguise the difference as well as protect the surface (see "Chairs," Windsor). If a piece has Indian red or old blue paint that is obviously the original finish of the piece, no attempt should be made to remove it. This can be determined by examining it where it is worn.

Some pieces were painted inside and out. If it's original (see "Paint," Chapter 27), don't remove it. All finishes including paint will fade from light, sun rays or other external elements. The amount of fading can help in determining the age of the piece.

Does any other color show through in worn spots or on the bottom? Check the bottoms of chairs, drawers, chests to see if other colors show through. If not, and there are no signs of clear finishes at the edges, it is in all probability original. Leaving this paint on increases the value considerably and often dates the piece.

Curly maple was often painted or stained to imitate mahogany, but has since become rare. Whichever finish you decide to keep depends on whether you prefer woods or original finish.

Pieces which are not solid hardwood are often veneered. Veneer is a wafer-thin layer of fine wood glued to a less expensive wood. The earliest veneer (c. 1700) was as much as one-tenth-inch thick. By 1850, it had thinned down to one-fiftieth-inch thick. Depending on the style of the piece, it is usually safe to say that the thicker the veneer, the older the piece.

Some pieces were finished with a combination of boiled linseed oil and turpentine. This oil finish is not difficult to determine.

1710

Lacquer or japanning in vogue. Can be distinguished from later lacquer pieces because of raised surface.

1750 on

Finish painted to simulate wood grain.

1790

Lacquered pieces have flat surface, coat of varnish over painted designs in gilt or colors.

1820–40

With the popularity of Hitchcock, stenciling came into style.

1850–80

Painted cottage pieces became the vogue. Over the years, this original finish may have been covered with many coats of enamel. Find an inconspicuous spot (at the bottom of a drawer or door) and scrape a small area to see if other colors appear.

1820–40

Empire pieces (see "Styles," Chapter 35) were made of poplar, then stained with varnish or veneered. Although some of the better pieces had hardwoods in drawer fronts and tops, the rest of the piece was usually veneered.

1840–1901

Varnish was generally the popular finish during the Victorian period, a carry-over from the Empire era. With the advent of steam and water power, the manufacturing of furniture gained momentum. Less care was paid to the refinement of raw lumber, and heavy layers of varnish provided the desired finish.

CHAPTER 18

Hinges

Early hinges show hammer or rasp marks and because they were made by hand, no two are exactly alike. Look for blacksmith charm, hand forging and thin edges.

Early 1700s through mid-1800s

Strap hinge. Most common to chests. Flat strap of iron folded over a pin and hand forged to form one end. Other end is made in same fashion. Wood screws used to attach. Widely used after 1725, throughout the 1700s through mid-1800s, surpassing H and HL hinges.

1700–1825

H hinge. Hand forged and showing hammer marks. Clinched. Used on early cupboards and doors. Some have fleur de lis, heart ends, circles, arrows, snakes and gooseheads. Earliest are applied with nails; later with screws.

HL hinge. Used during the same period but ususally with nails. In early 1800s, cut nails and screws were used to join them to the piece.

1700–50

Staple or snipe hinge. Looks like two thick iron bobby pins linked through the heads or tops. The ends form two sharp long points which are inserted into the boards and clinched back into the wood. Also called clinch or cotter pin hinge, they never gained popularity and declined after mid-1700s. Used in six-board chests, desk lids, cupboard doors. Seldom found on tables.

1700–1800

Rat-tail hinge. Predominantly on Pennsylvania and New York cupboards. Sometimes handmade nails clinched in place, but usually used rivets held with iron washers on inside of door. Doors could be removed by lifting them from the stationary pin mounted on the frame.

1725–50

Butterfly hinge. Held in place with short handwrought iron nails which were then clinched. Outer ends thinner than central section. Used first on drop-leaf tables and door hinges.

1725

Handmade rectangular table hinge. Earliest had square end wood screws. During the later 1700s it became more exact and smoother in appearance with fewer hammer marks. Early drop-leaf tables have as many as three or four to each joint.

1800 on

Heavy rectangular cast-iron hinge. Thick, brittle, usually has three holes on each side, sometimes four. Hand-wrought. Attached with square-end screws.

1820 on

Machine-made rectangle hinge. Also brittle, ends curve into circle over pin. No longer hand finished. Use continues to present day.

CHAPTER 19

Interior

Once you become familiar with what you're looking for, interiors of antiques can be read as easily as a doctor examines an X ray.

Repairs, replacements, rearrangements, wear and age are all there waiting to be recognized for what they are. No matter what has been done to the outside, some clue will remain on the interior for you to find.

Old wood turns gray with age, a condition impossible to reproduce. Make sure this gray is the same tone and color throughout.

Look for restoration. If some part appears to be a

73

different tone, find out what has been replaced or rearranged and why.

Look for age and wear. A table, for instance, may be sanded slick on the outside, but bear all the signs of wear and age on the interior. For instance, where the drawers slide on the runners, are the runners worn? Have they been replaced? If so, is the bottom of the drawer also worn? (See "Drawers," Chapter 13.)

Is the secondary wood in the drawers the same as the interior secondary wood? When expensive woods were used (i.e., mahogany, walnut, cherry, curly maple, etc.), American cabinetmakers would normally use either pine or poplar as a secondary wood in sections that did not show. From Virginia southward, pine was favored because of its abundance. Makers north of Virginia used poplar for the same reason. When you see oak as a secondary wood, you can almost rest assured it is an English piece.

Check the width of the boards and thickness of the wood. Older pieces were made with wider and thicker boards, oftentimes as wide as thirty inches because trees were quarter sawed. One side was then used against the other to prevent warping.

How is it joined? (See "Joining," Chapter 20.)

Are the corners of the piece dovetailed together top and bottom? This was done on better older pieces to keep the boards straight on the ends and in the middle. Dovetailing was the only method used to fasten the boards together to construct the piece. Nails were scarce and hard to come by.

Another thing to look for is dust separators, pieces of wood placed between the drawers to prevent dust from seeping through. Few pieces were made with dust separators after 1810. If it has them, it was probably made before then.

Look for saw marks (see "Backs," Chapter 2).

If the antique has more than one piece (i.e., corner cupboard), both pieces should feel and smell the same inside. The interior wood should also be lighter than the unfinished back because it has not been exposed to air and dust.

Exceptions: Some woods like tulipwood and basswood, when kept out of light will stay light in color. Therefore, if everything else checks out as authentic and the inside wood appears light, this may be the reason why (see "Woods," Chapter 39). Pine, though, darkens considerably with age.

CHAPTER 20

Joining

Until 1725, furniture was made by turners and joiners. Country provincial joiners used native woods. They usually could not afford labels and sometimes impressed their names with a pressure stamp on the bottom of drawers, or on backboards and chair bottoms.

Wealthy joiners who made furniture for city dwellers and plantation owners used mahogany, walnut, cherry woods. They sometimes used labels.

Glue is rarely found in primitive furniture and never in very early pieces, as it was not invented until about 1750. Early furniture was held together by exact joining.

Chair legs were only partially seasoned, but the rungs always were. As the wood aged, the legs dried, making the rungs even tighter.

The mortise and tenon joint is found on early pieces and better pieces of later periods. Tenons two inches to four inches wide fit into a rectangular opening called a mortise.

A dovetail is a wedge-shaped joint (see "Drawers") cut in the shape of a dove's tail that fits a corresponding section. In early pieces, broad dovetails were fastened with nails of the period. Later dovetailing is more refined, machine made and grows progressively narrower up to 1900.

Dowels were usually made from hardwoods like ash, oak and hickory. Because early dowels were made by hand and shrink with age, they are not perfectly round. If a dowel *is* perfectly round, it is usually machine made. Some old dowels are oblong. All old dowels were driven in place without glue.

On flat items such as tables or large surfaces, requiring more than one board, a variety of methods were used:

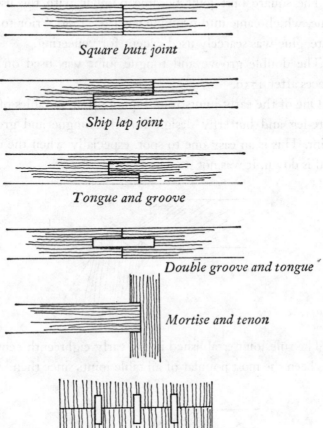

Square butt joint

Ship lap joint

Tongue and groove

Double groove and tongue

Mortise and tenon

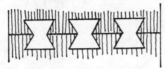

Doweled joint

Double butterfly joint

77

The square butt joint became popular with the use of glue, which came into prominence after 1780. Prior to this date, glue was scarcely used except for veneering.

The double groove and tongue joint was used on fine pieces after 1750.

One of the early joints found quite often on tables of the gate-leg and butterfly design was the tongue and groove joint. This is an easy one to spot, especially when the drop leaf is down. It was not used much after 1725.

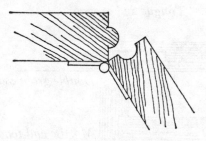

The rule joint established in the early eighteenth century has been the most popular of all table joints since then.

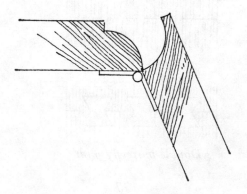

The square joint on tables is not common since most tables now in existence show the "rule joint." Occasionally a piece will be found with the square joint made by a local maker who avoided the effort of turning out a more difficult joint.

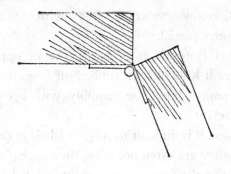

CHAPTER 21

Labels, Signatures

Few antiques carry a label, although one Delaware case piece has been found with as many as three labels. One of the best ways to become familiar with what early labels look like is by examining those in any of the shelf clocks made from 1800 on. If the label is pasted on the back, it is in all probability the label of the vendor or the store. The manufacturer usually pasted his label inside the front door on the backboard of the clock.

Country furniture makers could not afford labels, and although finer makers used them, the paper was inferior and usually deteriorated, falling off and sometimes leaving only a partial section. Sometimes close examination of a piece will show evidence of a lighter area where a label was once pasted.

If a label is found it is usually in an out-of-the-way place where it has not been rubbed off from wear or cleaning. The paper should be crumbly with age and have a dried-out texture.

One reason it is difficult to rely on labels in dating a piece is because they are often not what they appear to be. Many times what is thought to be a maker's label is actually a shipping label to the orginal owner. Labels can also be faked by using old paper, old print on stained paper, or transferred from something else. The most common way to fake a label is to cut out an ad from an old newspaper and glue it on.

A label may also be from the shop of the workman who restored the piece, the importer who imported it, or the dealer who sold it. Check the name and address on the label in old city directories to determine what it is.

Check the insides and sides of drawers for newer labels or metal stamps, all signs of reproductions. Factory-made oak furniture manufactured from 1890 on often had a label attached with four tacks, one at each corner, on the back of the piece, inside or under the drawer. This label was sometimes paper, but more often was of hard smooth cardboard and sometimes cut like a mailing tag. It contained the name and address of the manufacturer and sometimes the name and address of the merchant purchasing the furniture. Often this tag has been removed, leaving the tacks or holes.

From 1910 on, manufacturers began stenciling their names in black paint on the back of the piece or glued a yellow paper label with their name and address on the back of the piece or inside the drawer. Complete bedroom sets with as many as three to ten pieces often had only one label, and this was usually found on the back of the bed. To determine the exact date of manufacture, you can write to the Chamber of Commerce or historical society in the town and state listed, asking when that particular manufacturer was in business at that address.

Beware of labels using Olde English print. This is a new innovation. Older labels used simple script letters, usually with scrolled capitals, and the letters were round rather than square.

If, despite all these warnings, you feel the label is truly authentic, check the name in one of the directories of American furniture makers. Then, after you find his address (if it is not listed on the label), check it out in city indices of the period. Because makers moved to larger quarters as business improved, the address on the label can actually pinpoint the year the piece was made.

Instead of labels, some makers inscribed their mark or signature on an undersurface, but this is rare and only found on exceptional and high quality pieces. Other makers used pressure irons to mark their names on a piece. Branding or burning his name with an iron when found was usually done by an owner to prevent theft.

Large case pieces were made in large shops by many workers, each of whom had a different specialty. A signature when found could be that of a craftsman and not the designer or shop owner. If a signature is found, check *Directory of American Furniture Makers* for authentication.

Lambert Hitchcock, who made the Hitchcock chair, not only stenciled designs on chairs but his signature as well. When found, an authentic Hitchcock signature is an excellent way of dating a piece. During the first stage of manufacture (1818–29) his chairs were signed "L. Hitchcock, Hitchcocksville, Connecticut. Warranted," under the seat. From 1829 to 1843, he went into partnership with Arba Alford and during this period, chairs were stenciled "Hitchcock, Alford & Co., Warranted." In 1843, the partnership dissolved and Hitchcock signed his chairs from then until 1852, "Lambert Hitchcock, Unionville, Connecticut." His former partner continued making chairs with his brother as partner and their chairs were signed "Alford & Company."

Hitchcocksville, site of the first Hitchcock factory, is now Riverton, and chairs made there today use the first stencil with the "N" reversed. To differentiate between today's chair and the original, "H.C.Co." is now added under the front of the seat.

CHAPTER 22

Look

Stand back and look at an antique. Is it balanced? Does it all hang together like it should? If there is one part that doesn't, start your examination there.

Does the top "fit" the bottom? Is it the same style all over?

With age, antiques develop what is known as patina. This is a blush or glow of old age. Wallace Nutting, whom some consider the dean of antiquarians, thought the whole subject of patina was overdone, but once you recognize patina, it's a good quality to search for.

Antiques develop a transparent depth that glows in color, growing darker with age when kept in an ordinary room, but fading to a lighter tone when exposed to the sun. Inferior unfinished surfaces will range in color from honey to dark parchment, but inside or out, the patina should be even in color.

Paint mellows and fades with age.

Look for signs of wear where feet and hands rested on chairs, or feet kicked the legs of tables. Examine the top surface with a magnifying glass for tiny scratches resulting from years of dusting and usage.

Sharp edges become rounded with age. The lips of drawers become uneven or broken. Pieces of inlay disappear. Cracks appear in veneer. Tables that started round become slightly oval as the wood across the grain shrinks.

Many old rectangular tables were cut from extremely wide boards. With age, these edges curl or warp as they dry out.

Look for machine marks. If you find too many, too much restoration has taken place or else it is a reproduction. (See "Fakes" and "Repairs and Replacements.")

Has the piece been cut down from a larger piece? Look at the joinings, the base of the table as well as the top and bottom. Has any new wood been added? Try to determine why.

Have the moldings been repaired or replaced? Early moldings were fragile and nailed with small handmade brads or wood pins. Over the years, the moldings sometimes warp away from the piece, necessitating repair or complete removal. Are the moldings too wide and added to cover a bad repair or a marriage between two separate pieces of furniture? Is it the same wood or has it been stained and/or rubbed with something to make it look the same tone? If so, examine the interior closely to see what it is covering up.

CHAPTER 23

Legs

The creation of furniture brought with it many types of legs.

The cabriole leg used from 1700 on was used generously in Queen Anne and Chippendale periods. A curved leg with rounded knee and incurved ankle, it originated in Italy and is supposed to look like the rear leg of a leaping goat.

Normal straight legs vary in length and usually conform to the dimensions of the piece to which they are attached.

Turned legs derive their name from the "turner" or lathe operator who once made them. They are found in many designs such as the inverted cup of the William and Mary period and the spiral of the Sheraton era.

Cluster-column legs are a unique arrangement of several columns placed together. Not commonly found.

Fretted legs represent a series of fretwork carved into the straight leg (mostly Chippendale pieces) or fretwork cut and later applied to the leg.

Grooved legs were popular during the Chippendale

period. Grooves were cut creating channels or hollows on the surface of the wood.

Tapered legs can be square or round which grow gradually smaller from the top to the bottom. Most popular during the Hepplewhite period.

Splayed or raked legs are not set in a vertical position but placed at an angle or slant. The front legs project to the side and the rear legs to the back and sides.

Concave legs curve inward in a concave line. This is probably a Sheraton creation (1810) and later copied by Duncan Phyfe.

Round legs are turned legs which are often reeded or fluted.

See also: "Tables," "Feet," "Case Pieces."

Puritan

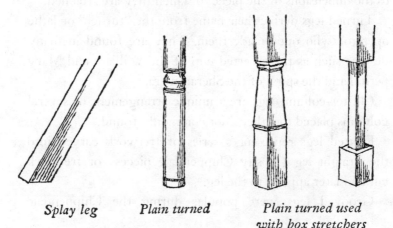

Splay leg   *Plain turned*   *Plain turned used
                                              with box stretchers*

William and Mary (1690–1725)

Trumpet   Inverted cup

Queen Anne

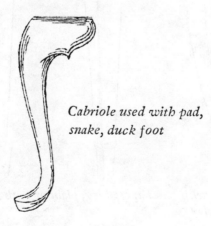

Cabriole used with pad,
snake, duck foot

87

Chippendale

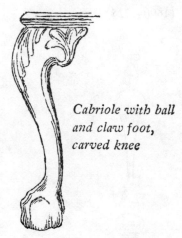

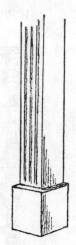

Cabriole with ball
and claw foot,
carved knee

Marlborough or straight leg,
sometimes with reeding
or fretwork

Hepplewhite

Tapered leg with
outward splay

Tapered leg, plain or with spade foot

88

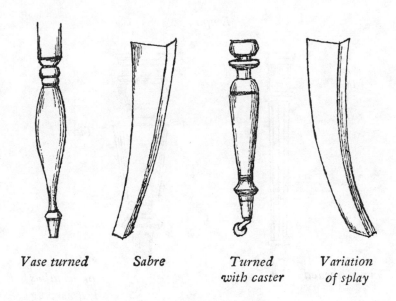

Vase turned   *Sabre*   *Turned with caster*   *Variation of splay*

Duncan Phyfe

(*Note:* 1810 Sabre leg reeded, but by 1850, curve became elaborately carved lion's paw or cornucopia, but much heavier.)
Sash-cornered front legs set at 135° angle to front and side rails.

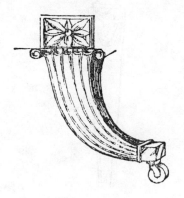

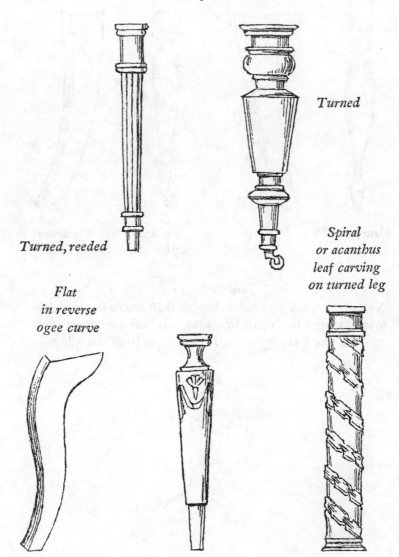

Empire

Turned

Turned, reeded

Spiral
or acanthus
leaf carving
on turned leg

Flat
in reverse
ogee curve

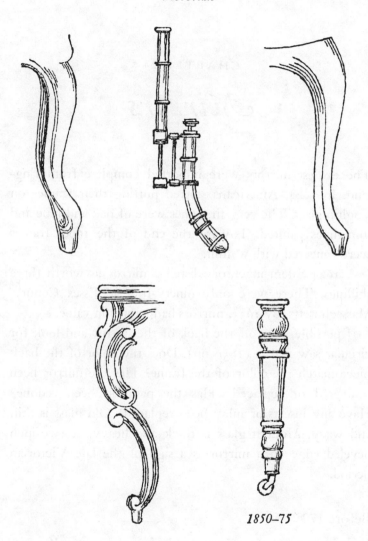

1850–75

CHAPTER 24

Mirrors

The earliest mirrors were imported complete from England. In 1644, Americans started putting their frames on English glass. The very first ones were of oak and pine and sometimes painted. Toward the end of the 1600s frames were veneered with walnut.

A 1644 Salem inventory listed a mirror as worth three shillings. There were only ninety-four in Essex County, Massachusetts. By 1655, mirrors had tripled in value.

If possible, take off the back of the mirror and look for circular saw marks (1850 on). Does the color of the back piece match the color of the frame? Has the mirror been resilvered or replaced? Has the painting been redone? Have any inserts or inlay been replaced? Old glass is thin and wavy. Modern glass is thick and heavy. A two-inch beveled edge on a mirror is a sign of the late Victorian period.

Before 1725

Cresting is a separate piece attached to the frame. If cresting is all one piece with the frame, it was made after 1725.

MIRRORS

1725–65

Early Queen Anne mirrors were made in two sections because glass was rare. No molding covered the joint of the two sections. They were framed in a simple molding arch with a cyma or S-shaped curve on top.

1725–50

Upper section of glass sometimes engraved with a floral pattern or heraldic device.

1729–50

Japanning in vogue. Similar to enamel or lacquer in a glossy finish, sometimes with gold patterns.

1730 on

Inner border carved and gilded.

1732 on

Pier glass, a long elegant mirror, was used between windows.

1750–80

Chippendale mirrors became one sheet of glass with fretwork on top and bottom. Sometimes a gilded ornament (shell, acorn, phoenix bird) was set in top section. American mirrors of this type are longer than English, which are broader. On English mirrors, the backboard fits *inside* the frame. On American pieces the backboard is larger than the size of the opening of the frame and nailed to the frame to protect the back of the mirror. Mahogany was the favorite wood. This is often a faded, golden color.

Another form of Chippendale mirror was the architectural mirror, sometimes called a Constitutional mirror. Larger and heavier than the typical Chippendale mirror, it has a scroll top, gilt ornament, hanging fruit along the sides. One way to distinguish between a period mirror and a reproduction, in addition to those mentioned, is that on old mirrors the hanging fruit at the sides is carved of wood, while reproductions use plaster molds.

1780–1800

Hepplewhite mirrors became more delicate, elegantly thin, with less wood visible and more gilt. The most common form showed an urn at center top with a flower spray.

1795–1820

Sheraton mirrors became flattened on the top, with even more gilt. They sometimes had columns at the sides, with overhanging cornice. The tabernacle style has a row of balls under the top panel. This model is also called a Constitution mirror because of a painted panel at the top often containing a picture of the frigate. (For how to date other painted panels, see "Clocks," reverse painting on glass.) Other Sheraton mirrors used acorns between cornice and mirror.

1800–20

During this period, the Girandole convex mirror appeared.

Round simple wood frame, often gilded, had raised mirror glass.

1810 on

Heavy ball ornament, twisted rope moldings.

1840–65

The rectangular ogee mirror made of natural wood became popular. Sometimes made with a gold liner.

1840–70

Mantel mirrors. Square dimension with curved top, elaborate rococo detail of flowers, fruits. Made for mansions, elaborate town houses.

1840–75

Oval gilded with carving top and bottom of fruit or flowers. Softwood with gesso finish.

1855–75

Pier mirror. Tall and thin, designed to hang over pier table in hall or between windows.

1860–80

Cottage mirror, curved top, square bottom. Softwood stained or gessoed to look like more expensive woods.

1865–75

Oval gilt on black walnut.

1865–75

Rustic mirror. Arched top and sides carved to look like branches, leaves. Black walnut.

1870–85

Eastlake rectangular mirror. Molded cornice overlapping sides, small geometric details with burl veneer trim, gilt scrolling.

CHAPTER 25

Moldings

The term "molding" has two meanings: a design cut into an edge (i.e., table top or door frame) or, more generally, a piece of wood added by nails or glue (i.e., cornice on top of a cupboard). A molding which projects is usually added. One that is indented is cut into the wood. Reeding and fluting are actually carving.

Early moldings were made by a cabinetmaker who usually had a range of thirty planes. They were simple and held in place with small handmade iron brads until 1840. They were never glued.

Moldings on early pieces were made at low speed by a wheel that was operated by a horse or treadmill. This left marks on the turned sections, slight undulations or ridges made by the chisel or turning skewer.

In the early eighteenth century with the advent of various methods of power (waterwheels, hand-operated units, etc.), more designs began to appear.

The most primitive and early molding was the arch type.

Later, the double arch came in with the canal mold.

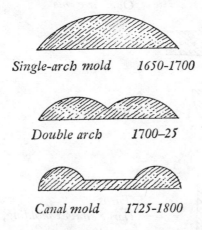

Single-arch mold   1650-1700

Double arch   1700–25

Canal mold   1725-1800

Many of the early moldings were creations and adaptations of the individual cabinetmaker. There were no set standards. Very often they would change the cut to adapt to a particular piece and its styling.

Modern usage has standardized all of the various shapes in order to conform with simplicity in production. Moldings of every description are available in pine and redwoods. If a modern cabinetmaker prefers walnut, cherry or mahogany moldings, he must make them by hand or special order them.

Other common moldings are:

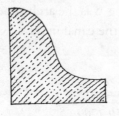 *Dentil*
(looks like row of rectangular teeth)

 Ogee or cyma

 *Thumbnail*

 Torus
(large convex molding, i.e.,
Empire acorn)

Quarter round

 *Bead*

See also: "Periods," "Styles," "Woods."

CHAPTER 26

$\mathcal{N}ails$

Early period pieces contain handmade or hand-forged nails. They have a rough uneven surface, and although they bend easily, do not break. They are highly resistant to rust and dampness.

The very earliest handwrought nails were imported from England, but after iron deposits were located in America toward the middle of the seventeenth century, records indicate that our smiths began making nails.

These nails, which vary in length from one inch to six inches, were made with two kinds of heads: oblong (showing the marks of the hammer and called mushroom or rosebud) and flat or folded (which resemble an elongated T). Moldings used the tiny heads while H, HL and butterfly hinges used large circular nails.

Any antique with hand-forged nails can be dated with certainty before 1790 because the cut-nail era began in 1785 with the invention of Ezekiel Reed's cut-nail machine. But the cut nail did not catch on immediately, so if a piece has all handmade nails, you can probably stretch this

time period up to 1815 when the earliest form of machine-made nails came into wider use.

This early machine nail was cut from sheets of iron by a
machine which left a cutting mark along the shank edge
and fashioned a square head. These "cut" nails are not as
precise as the later machine nail, but were widely used until
about 1875.

1785

Ezekiel Reed's cut-nail machine invented.

1810

Tack machine invented.

1815

Early machine-made nails came into wider use.

1820

Screw cutting machine appeared on scene.

1870

Cut- (or cold) nail machines first produced. Wide part of
shank was driven parallel with wood grain to avoid split-
ting. These nails are not as tough as older handmade nails
because they have not been exposed to intense heat required for hand forging. Usually square on point.

CHAPTER 27

Paint

Painted pieces must be examined more closely than finished because paint is often used to cover up repairs or replacements.

Paint covers a multitude of sins including:

1. cracks
2. breaks
3. repairs
4. nails
5. inferior wood
6. replaced wood
7. lost veneer

Old paint was made from natural pigments, using berries, nuts and barks for dyes. It is not bright and has natural tones. It also loses its oil with age, making it brittle and easy to shatter. When hit with a hard object or scraped, it powders or comes off in tiny chips.

New paint is softer and less like glass. When scraped, it comes off in strips and narrow ribbons.

Older pieces should have layers of paint in the same order on all sections. When rubbed down to the wood or scraped in a single area, the paint should appear like rings in the diameter of a tree. If, in cleaning off paint, you discover this doesn't bear true, you can determine which sections have been replaced or repaired.

If you are satisfied with the color, check under the chair seat where the legs are joined or at the bottom of a drawer, etc., and you will find a record of what colors are under the existing paint.

If after examination you are fairly certain the piece has its original paint and possesses enough worn spots showing wood with no traces of other colors, go no further. The original paint greatly enhances the charm and value of the piece.

If the piece is newly painted and every surface is thoroughly coated (bottom and interior), watch out. Something is being covered up.

See also: "Fakes," "Finish."

CHAPTER 28

Periods of Workmanship and Influence

There were roughly three periods of American craftsmanship: early, middle and late.

Early pieces were handcrafted, sturdy, simple in design, made for everyday wear.

Pieces from the middle period were a combination of handcraftsmanship and machine work.

Those of the later period were made completely by machine. The only handwork required was in the assembly of the finished piece.

Early- and middle-period pieces were individually made according to the creative design of the individual craftsman. The workmanship of the piece usually reflects whether it was made in the city or country.

The finest workmen and largest makers were located in cities because that is where the market was. Wealthy patrons could afford to pay more. The maker could use better woods, more elaborate turnings and afford more time in making the piece. City pieces were more formal, made of dark expensive woods like mahogany, had more carving, inlay, fluted reeded corners and a greater degree of refinement in the molding.

Masters made only the best. A craftsman like Duncan Phyfe did not have to spend time making a five-hundred-dollar piece of furniture when he had clients clamoring for one-thousand-dollar items.

Country craftsmen copied city pieces, usually in less expensive woods like pine or poplar, sometimes using a combination of woods which they then covered with paint. Because they lacked the skill or the tools, their furniture was less intricate, more informal and not as pure in line.

More country pieces exist today because then, as now, a greater percentage of the population belonged to the lower and middle classes. The number of wealthy clientele commissioning the finer pieces was few, which is one reason why today as then they command a higher price.

If you were to define these periods of workmanship and influence by dates, they would fall into the following categories:

1730–80

Everything made by hand. After the Revolutionary War, a degree of overseas influence became evident in the use of the treadle lathe, which eliminated making turnings by hand.

1730–80

All nails were hand forged, no two are exactly alike.

PERIODS OF WORKMANSHIP

1800 on

Workmen began to fabricate ways of doing things other than entirely by hand.

1830 on

Primitive machine nails appeared on the scene (see "Nails," Chapter 26).

1850 on

All parts, including screws, were made by machine.

After the Civil War, the machine influence appeared in almost all furniture. With each passing year until 1900, furniture showed more mechanical influence.

Exceptions: After 1900, handmade pieces were rare. When found, they are usually the work of a modern craftsman creating a good reproduction and should be judged on merit alone. If the piece appeals to you, try to judge its age and accept it as it is.

See also: "Joining," "Nails," "Screws," "Styles," "Woods."

CHAPTER 29

Regional Differences

Once you can recognize regional differences in your own area, you will begin to appreciate variations in other parts of the country and the world.

Visit your local library and see what collections they have or know about. Go on house tours. Visit the museum and historical society. It's much easier to remember what antiques are used for when you see them in room settings. Local auctions are an excellent place to examine pieces firsthand.

Workmen in each region had reasons for making things differently. Once you become aware of the differences in workmanship and design you will be able to spot rare pieces that would otherwise go unnoticed. What commands a high price in one area often goes cheaply in another.

For instance, American Chippendale furniture is a more conservative, classical version of the English rococo in style. The Charleston makers were the closest in appearance to the English in ornamentation and fretwork. But English chairs had higher ears on the back. English carving was done in a more flowing manner, whereas the American was more crisp. American ball and claw feet were bolder and more varied.

The New England ball and claw had one talon resting on the ball.

But the Philadelphia ball and claw had the ball held firmly within the claw. The foot was more squat than any other American Chippendale style and proportionately smaller.

The New York Chippendale foot had a square ball with the claw following the same shape.

The Newport makers made a loose claw with a tendon over an oval ball. If you look closely, you can see light between the ball and claw.

Massachusetts ball and claw feet had hairy claws on chairs, desks and chests.

Splat-back chairs made in New York had the thickest splat. New England's were more slender, while Philadelphia's were the most sophisticated. Shakers made slat backs from 1770 on, but always kept them simple, functional, with no ornament and used light native woods.

New England Queen Anne chairs were restrained in style, while Philadelphia Queen Anne chairs are noted for their shell decorations and stretchers.

On both Queen Anne and Chippendale chairs made in New York, the carving on the knees is deep with an area of crosshatching in triangular shape at the center of the knee top.

Hepplewhite pieces made in Baltimore used more inlay than those made in New York.

Sheraton and Hepplewhite furniture made in Ohio and Mississippi is simpler and heavier than that made in New England or Pennsylvania. It is also sometimes thirty years behind in style. If the history of the piece clearly shows that it was made in Ohio or Mississippi, this must be taken into consideration in determining its age.

Blanket chests also differed. The Pennsylvania Germans usually painted flowers, birds, hearts, etc. on theirs in neat panels.

The Scandinavians curved the top lid, tapered the sides and did free handpainting all over the exterior.

New York case pieces are usually straight across the front with chamfered and fluted corners.

There was also a great difference in the use of secondary woods. New York State usually used poplar and sometimes pine, as did Pennsylvania. From Virginia southward, the interior was almost always pine.

Places close to Philadelphia had completely different methods of workmanship because of ethnic backgrounds and expertise of the craftsman. For instance, Lancaster designs were carved out of wood where Philadelphia's were applied. Philadelphia pieces had a more academic line, whereas Chester County furniture had flower designs, inlay and more freedom of interpretation.

During the Chippendale period, Philadelphia chairs omitted the stretcher, had a narrower seat one inch higher. New England chairs are more angular, with a sharp rise on the knee, a force form foot with a deep back behind the ankle.

Maryland makers used walnut in Puritan span, a four-petal flower inlay on Chippendale and Hepplewhite pieces, and their Hepplewhite chairs had heart- and oval-shaped backs.

New England cabinetmakers had a reputation for a throbbing surface movement, serpentine front, tight control of line and sometimes silver brasses.

Delaware pieces are noted for a terrapin (turtle) inlay.

The bombé or swell base was made only in Boston and along the North Shore, and only for the wealthy.

New Orleans pieces used cherry as a secondary wood.

Tulipwood and poplar were the major secondary woods in New England chairs.

Charleston tea tables were made without the bird cage in the tilt top.

Furniture of New York origin has a winged splat in the back. Also associated with New York furniture is the sausage turning and an orangey color used on children's toys.

See also: "Interiors."

CHAPTER 30

Repairs and Replacements

Pieces with structural or major deficiencies should not be considered, as only minor problems can be corrected. Very often these can be left unattended without lessening the value of the item. Slight wear scars will enhance the charm of an old piece. Complete refinishing should be done only when no other alternative is available and then only by one proficient in the field.

Antiques are often described as being in the original condition, rough, restored, reconstructed or refinished.

Original condition or finish means that it appears much today as it did when first made except for wear.

When described as "in the rough," it needs work of some kind. It may have a poor finish or half its parts may be missing. If the piece only needs to be cleaned, reglued and rubbed down, "in the rough" is a better way to buy it than if it has been "skinned" past the original finish, stained a different color or remade into something else. If an antique has been skinned (sanded past the patina), it is worth half as much and only unsophisticated buyers will consider purchasing it.

Refinished usually means resurfaced. Hopefully, the piece has been refinished by a person who did not remove the marks of age.

Restored can mean that missing parts have been replaced. If this is the case, 90 per cent of the original should still be there. Replacements should be made of the same kind of wood.

Reconstructed can mean a pig in a poke that is neither fish nor fowl. Chances are that it is no longer an antique.

Anything less than 90 per cent of the original piece is a reconstruction and no longer an antique by professional standards.

Table

If it contains the original frame and legs but the top and both drops have been replaced, it is no longer an antique. However, using a drop leaf to repair or replace a damaged top and then adding a new drop leaf is permissible if the aggregate repair is no more than 10 per cent.

Chair

Permissible to add or replace feet, caning, chair seats, a rocker. However, if the arms have been cut off (which sometimes happens when one has been damaged), it loses its value.

Cupboard

Permissible to add or replace damaged feet if replacements are in keeping with the period of the cupboard, and if old wood is used, it is considered restoration rather than reconstruction. If paneled doors have been replaced with glass, the piece is no longer in its original state and should be sold as a piece of furniture and not as an antique.

One-drawer stands

If the top or a drawer has been replaced, it detracts from the value 50 to 60 per cent.

Mirrors

Permissible to replace glass. Repairs to frame should not be noticeable and of minor quantity.

Drawers

Replacement of pulls, repairs to lip and runners are permissible. However, when old drawers are rebuilt into a new frame, the piece is not an antique.

Split pieces

A cupboard top sometimes is sold as a "hanging cupboard" or the top of a chest-on-chest is made into a separate piece with top and feet added. This is considered an improved rather than a true antique. If this is the case, the buyer should be informed by the seller.

CHAPTER 31

Screws

Hand-finished screws have rough, coarse threads. The screwdriver slot is uneven and usually off center. The end has a flat surface instead of a point.

Those made by machine are very much like our modern screws. Screw making was in full force by 1850.

Screws will not always act as a guide to age because they were often saved and reused. However, if you are certain a piece contains the original screws and they are early, for authenticity's sake keep track of exactly which screws go into each piece of hardware. If for any reason the piece needs restoration and the screws must be removed, it is wise to attach them to a diagram showing their exact position so that they can be returned to their original holes.

1700–25

Drop-leaf tables with tongue and groove joints (see "Joining") had hinges attached with small nails, sometimes clinched on topside.

1725 on

After rule joint appeared, hinges applied with rough hand-made screws with blunt tips that needed holes drilled before insertion.

1750 on

Screws used more, but usually to fasten table tops to frames, tops to candlestands and between tripod legs to prevent spreading.

1815

Machine-made screws first appear, smoother in workmanship, with flat ends.

1830

Full-threaded handmade screws with gimlet or pointed end.

1850

Machine-made screws with gimlet ends, the beginning of the screw as we know it today.

CHAPTER 32

Sideboards

Sideboards began as side tables. They eventually grew into five separate pieces: a table, with two pedestals on each end on which two urns rested. These five pieces then became three (a table with drawers plus two urns); eventually becoming one, which was called a sideboard. The first one-piece sideboard appeared about 1780.

1785–1800

Hepplewhite sideboards were usually made of mahogany with inlay. Straight or serpentine fronts with concave ends. Their square-tapered legs sometimes ended in spade feet. Handles were brass, oval or round in shape. American Hepplewhite sideboards are more vertically slender than English with less ornamentation.

1800–20

Sheraton sideboards became deeper in height, and their fronts, rather than being concave like the Hepplewhite period, curved into convex ends. Their legs became shorter, round, turned and were often reeded or fluted; columns and legs project from the front.

1820–40

Empire pieces were topped with mirrors, marble, or were decorated with ormolu (a combination metal made of copper and zinc). Large, massive, they were usually made of softwood covered with hardwood veneers. The overhanging top contains one or two drawers with two cupboard doors underneath. There is sometimes an arrangement of doors and drawers down the center of the front. Corner columns, either plain or carved with acanthus leaf pattern, terminate in either carved paw feet with acanthus-carved knees or ring-turned legs with ball feet. Wood mushroom knobs.

1840 on

Victorian period. Heavy carving, oak and softwoods used. Machine-made metal handles, glass knobs or wooden handles carved in shape of fruit, nuts and leaves (see "Brasses"). Later Victorian period pieces were topped with mirror flanked by top and side shelves.

Exceptions: New England sideboards in all periods were often made of maple and cherry. Pennsylvania and southern pieces were sometimes walnut. Inlay was usually made from satinwood or maple.

1790–1830

Huntboards, a southern innovation, were originally made for buffet eating after the hunt. They started out as a simple slab of wood on four-foot tall legs without drawers. As they grew shorter and gained drawers, they became more formal and moved from the back hall into the dining room. They can be found in simple country pieces or modified Hepplewhite and Sheraton styles.

1750–1840

Sugar chest, another southern innovation, looks like a short blanket chest on legs. Usually divided into bin with lid on top, with bottom drawer with locks to protect sugar, coffee, tea and spices. Wooden, brass or glass knobs, turned or square tapering legs.

See also: "Backs," "Bottoms," "Brasses," "Feet," "Joining," "Legs," "Styles," "Turnings," "Woods."

CHAPTER 33

Smell

Although different kinds of wood differ slightly in smell, old furniture had a distinct musty fragrance that reminds you of an attic on a rainy day.

If a piece has been aged superficially (see "Fakes"), the color may look right, but the smell just won't be there.

Become familiar with the smell of antiques and when you're examining a piece, don't be afraid to pull out a drawer or open a door to make sure that it sniffs right.

CHAPTER 34

Sofas

Even experts have difficulty in determining whether a sofa or upholstered piece is period without examining its frame. Once a sofa or chair has been upholstered, this is difficult to do.

If a piece is of the period, it has in all probability been reupholstered several times. Each time new padding and springs have been added and the exposed wood sections refinished. This is the reason better dealers take pictures of upholstered antiques before, during and after. When there is something special under the upholstery, a seller *wants* you to know it.

But there are times when you find a sofa and it's not in an elegant shop and there are no "before" and "during" pictures to reassure you. What do you do then?

Examine exposed wood sections like arms, feet and legs for handcrafted details. Then picture the piece standing alone in a room of the period to which you think it belongs. (This takes a great deal of concentration, especially at an auction.) What does it say to you?

Good period pieces have a strong sense of presence. Their arrogant lines almost say, "Here I am. I'm pretty great. Take me home and build a room around me." We were going to add a chapter on how antiques talk, but we didn't think you'd believe it.

Basically, sofa styles are related in the following way:

1740–50

Queen Anne. Similar to Chippendale, but with Queen Anne feet. Upholstered backs with plain or scalloped tops. Settee made of two or three chair backs joined together.

1754–80

Chippendale. Similar to Queen Anne, but with ball and claw feet or straight legs. Sometimes upper frame is exposed and carved. Camel back.

1785–1810

Hepplewhite. Camel back of Chippendale period straightens out on back or has one simple curve. Wooden arm supports and tapered legs.

1795–1825

Sheraton-style sofas held the rectangular lines. The back is generally straight and frequently reeded. The legs follow the Hepplewhite style, but are round and tapered. Reeding is often found on the legs, but rarely on the stretchers. Wooden arm supports rather than upholstered.

1800–25

Duncan Phyfe. Had three styles from which to choose: Sheraton, Directory or Empire. Customers were given a choice and Phyfe made to their order. He was more interested in making money than creating new designs. Toward the end of his working career, he leaned heavily toward the Empire.

Best known for his sofa with a broad lyre back. Feet cornucopia shaped with casters or castered paws, or simulated animal feet with feathered wings.

1810–40

Empire sofas imitated the style already mentioned, but on a larger scale. The arms had roll-over curves. Feet were cyma curves, fat balls or animal feet. Made of fine mahogany in solids and veneers, they were well made, massive. Many exist today.

1840–1900

Victorian. Early Victorian sofas copied Empire styles, but after the Civil War what we know as the "typical Victorian sofa" came into being. Veneer on the skirt, cameo backs, an abundance of tufted upholstery, it usually came in sets with matching gentleman's and lady's chairs. It is often reproduced today.

CHAPTER 35

Styles

Style does not necessarily indicate age or date of manufacture. It is simply the pattern by which a piece of furniture is made. Only by examining each of its parts can you determine when it was made.

When an auctioneer or dealer says, "In the Chippendale style" (or manner, or period) it does not mean it is a Chippendale piece, yet all too often an unwary novice will take it to mean just that.

We have separated the styles into periods and years to show you what lines and features are related to each style. Only by examining the wood, screws, joining and other features can you determine the age of the piece.

1650–90

Puritan. Plain, paneled surfaces. Rugged, plain oak made to last, endure, survive. Early settlers did not have the time to be fancy. They owned little and had to share much. Their furniture imitated the English pieces they knew. Knobby, bulky, simple, but well proportioned. Oak, though durable, was difficult to carve. The carving was flat, but often painted or stained in black, blue, red and green to emphasize flat carving or bring out the molding on a chest. Pieces associated with this era are court cupboards (low cupboards on an open frame); press cupboards (lower section is closed with doors or made as chest of drawers to hold linens). Top looks like Grandma's Victorian sideboard except with recessed doors instead of mirrors.

Innovations: Chests of drawers, trestle tables, three-legged armchairs, trundle beds, drop-leaf tables.

1690–1725

William and Mary. American pieces of this period were less massive than the English, simple though somewhat baroque, with teardrop pulls, curved stretchers, ball or bun feet with inverted cup or trumpet knees. Settlers had more time during this period to add inlays, marquetry, scrolls and columns. Walnut was the favorite wood with walnut and burl veneers.

Innovations: Highboy, lowboy, higher bedsteads, gateleg table, inverted cup and trumpet knee, cabriole leg, drop handles, scalloped skirt, butterfly table, splay leg.

1725–50

Queen Anne. Furniture, though similar in line to William and Mary, became light and curvy with shell sunbursts, delicate pad feet. This was the beginning of japanning. Workmen used cherry and maple in addition to the walnut of the former period. Regional differences became more apparent. Veneers were less important as fine solid woods gained popularity. The walnut wood in earlier pieces was gradually replaced with imported mahogany.

Innovations: The scallop shell, drop-leaf table, corner chair, Windsors, dutch and club foot, japanning.

Transitional: Queen Anne chairs with ball and claw feet, tea or china table.

1754–80

Chippendale. In many ways, a continuation of the Queen Anne period, with a carry-over of the cabriole leg, but during this period, furniture makers began to let out all the stops and to try everything. Bamboo-type carving, fretwork, rococo carving, acanthus leaves, elaborately carved aprons and skirts on chairs, bombé fronts on chests, the straight leg, the molded bracket foot, the ball and claw foot, a pierced carved splat in the back of chairs, fluting, reeding. The simple shell of the Queen Anne period was replaced by complicated foliate patterns. There were Gothic, Chinese and French influences. Furniture was mostly of mahogany, some walnut pieces, and in New England, cherry.

During this period there were significant differences between the American and English furniture. The English chairs had higher ears on the back. English carving was done in a more flowing manner, whereas the American was more crisp. American ball and claw feet were bolder and more varied.

Innovations: Tripod tables, piecrust tops, secretary tops on desks, bookcases, chairs without stretchers.

Note: The Adam styles became popular in England at the time of the Revolutionary War. By the time things had returned to normal in the United States, Hepplewhite and Sheraton had come on the scene. Hepplewhite and Sheraton were both of the same classical period. Some say they cannot be separated. We prefer to. Although they were both adapters of the Adam style, there were differences.

1785–1810

Hepplewhite. Less carving. Legs became square and tapered with spade feet on finer pieces. Much inlay of tulipwood, holly and boxwood. Designs of sunburst, conche shell, bellflower, eagle. Flat brasses, usually oval and sometimes round, with designs of fruit, grain, eagles, temples, crocodiles, dogs, lions, serpents, deer, doves. Carvings featured plumes, wheat, leaves, eagle, thunderbolt. Veneer returned to popularity. Shield-back chairs had heart and oval variations.

Innovations: Card table; tea, side, Pembroke, pedestal and sofa tables; bureaus; tambour desks; China closets and sideboards.

1790–1820

Sheraton. More feminine-looking furniture with turned, reeded legs. More common woods come into use. Tables with lyre and vase pedestals. Furniture makers gain machine power. Fronts and sides are veneered in contrasting light and dark woods. Chair backs become more squarish with lyre designs. Chests have reeded or ringed legs, corner column supports with round tapering feet. Legs extend through entire piece as columns projecting at corners with reeded or turned decoration. Inlaid ovals, cartouches, vase forms. Carving of drapery festoons, wheat, thunderbolts or rosettes. Oblong brass pulls with bails, rosette knobs or lion head with hanging ring.

Wood: Mahogany with satinwood, cherry with fancy maple.

Innovations: Dressers with mirrors attached, fancy chairs, dining-room table leaves.

1794–1846

Duncan Phyfe. Much the same as Directory, Directoire, Classical. Sabre-shape front leg, back crossbar or splat of lyre or vase shape. Every line was curved except the seat. Sofas with broad lyre backs. Cameo leaves, wheat ears, sheaves of lightning.

Wood: Mostly mahogany.

Innovations: None.

1815–40

Empire. Large, bulky, heavy lines, cube and rectangular shapes made to correspond with the architecture of large homes being built. End of handcrafted furniture; beginning of mass production. Commercialization sneaking in. Radical change of style with downward sloping curves, paneled sides, concave-curved front legs, columns at sides, winged legs and animal feet. There was an accumulation of everything. Bold carving, much veneer, ogee molding, cyma curves. Fat ball feet or animal legs and paws. Solid vase-shape chair splat. Tables with round or octagonal center column resting on plinth. Early hardware: projecting round brass knobs stamped with eagle, George Washington or patriotic motif. Later: ring pull hanging from brass lion head.

Wood: Mahogany, cherry, fancy maples, softwood with red stain, rosewood.

Innovations: Sleigh bed, Recamier or Grecian sofa (see "Beds," day bed), Boston rocker.

1830–68

Early Victorian. Layers of layers on everything. Material hung in doorways, chairs were padded extra deep, marble was laid on top of wood, plaster was covered with tin and tile and inlay, houses with gingerbread. From 1841, the Gothic arch gained in popularity with trefoils, cusp finials, crotchet carvings. Machine sawing and planing combined with hand fitting and finishing.

Woods: Mahogany, walnut, with many Belter pieces in rosewood.

Innovations: Extension table, spool turnings, what-not shelves.

1868–1900

Late Victorian. A passion for elegance and an epidemic of splendor set in. Furniture was almost completely machine made in large factories, to the designs of the owners by largely unskilled workers. Very often the criterion was to make as much furniture as inexpensively as possible that could be shipped easily. Wardrobe and bookcases gained in popularity. Crests and gargoyles came into vogue. Furniture was produced in "sets" rather than individual pieces. Balloon backs on chairs. Hall stands did everything but walk with mirrors, bookshelves, seats and fancy hooks.

Woods: Oak, poplar, walnut, elm, birch, ash.

Innovations: Platform rocker, Morris chair, hall stands, roll-top desk, ottoman.

CHAPTER 36

Tables

In making early tables, joiners used as wide a piece of wood as they could find so that there would not be so many pieces to join. Over the years, these boards shrink with age, often leaving as much as three-eighths-inch separation between.

Run your hand over the top of a table. Old boards that were cut and dressed by hand are not flat. Look at the table in the right light and you will see the undulation. Lay a steel straight edge on top and you can see the difference.

The top edges of a table should be worn round. Tavern

tables with a stretcher base are also worn at the top of the stretcher where the feet rested.

If a table has a drawer, the stretchers on the opposite side will show less wear because most tables with drawers stood against the wall with the drawer side facing the room.

Round tables grow slightly oval over the years as wood shrinks. Sometimes there is as much as one half inch difference.

Measure the legs with a caliper. Whether they are round or square, they will shrink across the grain. Pegs in table tops also project above the top because of shrinkage.

1600s

Mostly oak, some pine and softwoods. Simple lines with chunky feet. Heavy construction with mortise and tenon joints. Mortise and tenon joint is found on all earlier pieces and on better pieces made in later periods.

c. 1650

Trestle table. The top, as long as eight feet, rests on trestles joined by a brace.

1670–1780s

Gate leg. Narrow table with large drop leaves supported on legs and stretchers that swing out. Top is round, oval, square or oblong when open.

1680

First record of drop-leaf table, called "falling leaves."

1690–1725

Chair table. Back pivots down to rest on arms of chair when in use as a table. Sometimes called a hutch table, especially when the box is too high to sit on.

1700–20

Rectangular table with four turned legs joined by stretchers. Often has a drawer in skirt below top.

1690–1725

William and Mary. Mixing table, similar to lowboy, with four joined legs connected by cross stretchers.

1725–50

Queen Anne. Rectangular tea tables with cabriole legs. Tilt top is introduced. Tilts vertically when not in use on tripod of legs. Smaller versions are candlestands. Most Queen Anne tables are small and delicate in proportion.

Game or card table. Folding top with two hinged halves that double over when not in use. Rear leg swings out to support leaves when open. Inside surfaces often covered with felt with depressions for chips or counters and a wooden area for candlestick.

1754–80

Chippendale. Rectangular tea tables are made in greater number. Acanthus leaf on legs and skirt, with edge of top also carved. Elaborate carving on baluster. Scrolled or scalloped edge known as piecrust. Introduction of bird cage under tilt tops, which enables them to turn for easier serving.

Edge on card or game table becomes carved. One side folds over the other or leans against the wall when not in use.

Introduction of Pembroke, a rectangular breakfast table with short leaves which are curved or have a rounded edge. Stretchers X-shaped.

Side table used as a server (predecessor of sideboards), sometimes has marble top. Library table, often with large leather inset panel, rounded edges; cabriole legs with ball and claw feet.

1785–1800

Hepplewhite. Banquet table in three sections, each with leaves, which are joined together with metal clips.

Introduction of dressing table, a version of the low chest. Oblong top, fewer drawers on legs with a mirror attached. Hinged central section opens to compartmented interior. Introduction of a library table which is used in the middle of the room with a central support replacing four legs.

Lamp or one-drawer stand to support oil lamps. Four legs replacing tripod for safety. Three-inch skirt holds drawer. Some made with two drawers.

Side tables designed high for use in halls and parlors as well as dining rooms for servers.

Sewing table with square or octagonal top. Drawer compartmented to hold sewing materials. Made of mahogany, maple, cherry and satinwood, a fixed bag hanging from the bottom holds sewing materials.

Pier table similar to card table, but with stationary legs and top in shape of a half circle or oblong.

1810–30

Sheraton. Sofa writing table new on scene. A long narrow table with short drop leaves at either end. Stretchers joining legs. Originally designed for being "near the sofa," modern usage puts it behind the sofa.

1794–1846

Duncan Phyfe used a lyre and harp as a center baluster, with low outcurved legs on casters, often with metal feet.

1800–20

Sheraton dining table similar to Hepplewhite, but with turned or reeded legs. Later tables made with pedestal bases with curved or splayed legs, paw feet, casters. Sometimes leaves were added in middle section. Tops extend to as much as fifty-six inches in width. Mostly mahogany.

The Sheraton Pembroke table had turned or reeded legs, casters; drop leaf had either straight, clover-leaf cornered or serpentine edge.

1805–20

Drop-leaf table set on pedestal in shape of urn, reeded globe or acanthus-leaf design columns. Legs curve outward

with reeding design or resemble animal legs carved to simulate fur. Casters. Mahogany.

1800–20

Card table similar to Hepplewhite, but with serpentine
corners, reeded legs, inlays of fruit, flowers and drapery.
Feet ring and ball turned or small brass feet with cups.
Other versions: acanthus carved baluster with four splay
legs; lyre baluster.

1800–20

Pier table. Similar in appearance to card table, but with stationary top, rounded front corners. Turned and tapered
legs with reeding. Mahogany with crotch-grain veneer.

1795–1820

Sheraton sewing tables came in many forms. Some, similar
to lamp tables, with workbag hanging underneath; others
with pedestal base supporting oval-shaped tambour reeded
top which hides sewing workbag. Earliest sewing tables
have four square tapering legs. Later examples have reeded
legs or baluster with four splay legs.

1820–40

Empire. Legs are more elaborately carved, often in
acanthus design, heavier in appearance. Paw feet become
more animal-like. Heavier with more veneer. Ogee-framed
mirrors are supported by cyma-curved uprights. Drawers

often have curved fronts, glass or wooden knobs. Skirts of tables are deeper to accommodate more drawers. Feet are small and turned; a flattened ball; or ornately carved paws with casters underneath.

1840–60

Lyre X-shaped trestle, full of cyma curves and branches with pendant finials where trestles join. Whorl feet. Mahogany, rosewood.

1840–65

Drop leaf supported by pull or pivot brackets in table rather than extra leg. Turned legs with small peg or bun foot. Walnut, cherry, maple or light woods stained brown and red. Dressing table of this period has simple lines, with drawer width of top with wood gallery top and sides. Shelf between legs in place of stretchers.

1840–70

Transitional period. Empire lines with Victorian fussiness. Molded edge, curved corners, valanced skirt. Extension table has concealed telescopic bed on which leaves rest with extra leg underneath for support. Beginning of the Victorian flowers and leaves carving. Marble tops with shaped edges. Turned pendant finials (sometimes with teardrops) hang from corners. Bulbous pedestal (sometimes in shape of ornate harp) set on rectangular molded base on low bracket feet or cyma-curved legs with carving and whorl feet.

1840–70

Pedestal extension table forty-four to sixty inches wide. Simple, round-looking all over, round top with round or octagonal hollow baluster, fat cyma feet. Earlier examples, mahogany and rosewood. Later, oak. Tilt top is similar in appearance but without skirt under top. Sometimes made in papier-mâché ornately painted in black lacquer. Vase-shape baluster support rests on circular base of wood or papier-mâché.

1840–70

Spool-turned legs. Earlier spools go to floor without feet. Later end in small peg or cyma curve. Earlier tops have square corners, later more curved.

1850–65

Louis XV, Belter influence. This furniture was made to impress. So ornate it looks like it is still growing. Medallions, hanging grapes, flowers, leaves, tendrils, cabriole legs, carved knees and ankles with whorl feet. Once you see it, you'll never forget it, nor did Scarlett O'Hara. Mahogany, rosewood, black walnut.

1865–80

Louis XVI. Toned-down version of XV period. Concave-molded edge on top, carved rosettes above turned legs. Vase and urn turnings, base or urn-shaped feet with H-shaped stretcher. Black walnut, ebonized maple.

1865–80

Renaissance. Era of the big dreamers. Nostalgic furniture made for big mansions and Gothic houses. Combination of Louis XV carving and round Victorian lines. Heavy in appearance with carved panels, scrolled bracket, cyma, whorl or trestle feet. More simple flower- and leaf-carved medallions. Usually black walnut.

1870–85

Cottage. Made in great quantity by machine. Simple turned legs, simple designs. Flat scroll-cut feet, plain skirts. Earlier examples are black walnut or natural finish with brown stain. Later were pine, oak, maple, ash.

CHAPTER 37

Taste

By taste, we do not mean discrimination, but buds—the same equipment you use for tasting food.

Early iron was made in a different manner. As mentioned in the chapter on "Fakes," the final test of an antique gun is taste. When saliva hits old iron, a sharp biting taste results that lingers on the tongue with a hollow drying effect.

Since no two individuals have the same body chemistry, no two will have the same reaction to metal. You can develop this sense only by trial and experimentation.

The best place to find the exact taste of old iron is on eighteenth-century Kentucky or Pennsylvania rifles. The metallic composition when tasted has a distinct flavor. After you've tasted an old gun, try a new one. Knowing the difference will add a new tool to your antique sleuthing: your tongue.

Once you recognize the taste of old iron-forged metal, taste can tell you whether something is old or a reproduction. The next time you are in doubt about an old lock, hardware or anything made of iron, make sure it's clean and then lick it.

Some experts say they can tell the difference in wood by the same method (i.e., pecan, cedar), but we think your nose would be a better barometer.

CHAPTER 38

Turnings

Turning is the shaping of wood, that part of furniture with a cylindrical shape (i.e., legs, feet, bedposts, chair rungs, spindles and arms). Turning was done by a craftsman called a turner in a shop called a turnery on a machine called a lathe.

Early lathes were made of wood, with arbors at each end to hold the wood in place. One arbor was stationary, while the other adjusted to the length of wood to be turned.

The earliest lathes were powered by man, with a foot treadle and belt like a sewing machine. Where excessive power was needed, a horse or oxen were used. As man's technology grew, water wheels were introduced and later, steam power. By the time of the Civil War, the majority of turning was done by mechanical power. Patterns were chiseled first by hand, and then by machine.

Woods favored for turning are walnut, mahogany, cherry and maple, and have been used in turnings of all periods.

There are thousands of turning styles. Although certain

turnings are associated with each period, variations of the basic styles exist in every period to the present day, with one exception: the intricate trumpet designs of the William and Mary period.

From the advent of turning in the 1500s up to 1700, turning was fairly primitive. Threads of the chisel marks show in furniture made during this period because they were not sanded out.

Most furniture of the Puritan period was of oak and because it is hard, is considered a chipping wood. As more English craftsmen came to this country and walnut came into vogue, turning came into style. During the William

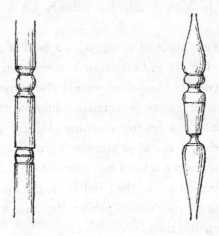

Simple, sturdy   *Icicle-type spindle*
usually found in chair backs
and between the arm and seat

During the Puritan span, turnings were simple, sturdy, usually oak, and were combinations of vase, ball, squared-off corners and icicles.

and Mary period, furniture makers let out all the stops and began to make turnings of ball and ring, spool and vase, and inverted trumpet shapes. Strangely enough, these were the first to fall by the wayside. They were difficult and expensive to produce. Cabinetmakers couldn't take the time or money to make them, and customers evidently didn't want to pay the additional cost.

Various forms of ball, vase, sausage, spool, twist (rope) and ring turnings exist in each period. Although you can't date a piece by the turnings, you can often tell where it was made and is a necessary link in adding up the total piece.

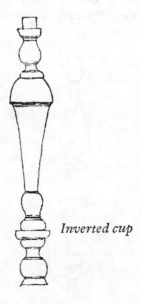

Inverted cup

During the William and Mary period (1690–1705), the inverted cup or trumpet-turned leg came into being. This style is represented as far down as 1720.

Spiral

An early use of the spiral or twisted rope effect has been found on chairs as far back as 1660–80 and became popular again during the Empire period.

Vase and ring

The vase and ring turning appeared during the period 1675–1700 and was also popular in Victorian pieces.

Curved bulb

The curved bulb (also called bulbous) appeared on Puritan furniture in 1650 and came into prominence again during the Empire period.

Spool

The spool turning was around in a simple form from 1675–1700 and gained tremendous popularity in the 1800s in cottage furniture in a more pronounced version.

Sausage

The sausage turning of 1675–1700 is usually associated with the Dutch and is repeated often in all periods of New York furniture.

Ball

The ball is seen in many variations from 1650 on and gained great popularity during the Empire period.

Turnings of each period are reflected in the architecture of houses in stair spindles and balusters, as well as fireplace mantels.

There are many turnings associated with certain regions (i.e., the sausage with New York and the ice-cream-cone shape of New England). Study the turnings of your region and you will soon be able to tell where a turning was made. Turners were great copycats, knew a good turn when they saw one and repeated it every chance they got.

CHAPTER 39

Woods

If you can distinguish one kind of wood from another, you can often tell where a piece was made, whether it is English or American and in what period it was made.

For instance, mahogany wasn't used in American furniture until 1750. The interior in English pieces is oak, but Americans usually used pine and poplar. Oak and chestnut are late Victorian woods.

Poplar is often disguised as something else, but once you recognize its green streaks, you can't be fooled again.

Primitive pieces were made with whatever kind of wood was plentiful. Sometimes early furniture (see "Chairs,"

Windsor) was made of many different kinds of wood and later painted (i.e., side rungs were made of pine and front rungs of maple and hickory). Clock gears were made of maple.

Hardwoods like walnut and cherry when found in wide boards would suggest an early piece. When wide trees are felled today, they are usually cut into veneer because wide wood is scarce and expensive. If you don't know the difference between hardwood and softwood, try lifting a piece of furniture made of hardwood and see. The best way to learn how woods differ in appearance is to visit your local lumberyard and get scraps to examine at home.

Certain woods were popular in certain periods. These are briefly:

1650–90

Puritan. Oak and pine. Flat carving, geometric details.

1690–1720

William and Mary. Beginning of lacquer, burl walnut or maple, plain unpaneled with dovetail joinings.

1720–50

Queen Anne. Walnut, maple or cherry. Beginning of pad, drake and Spanish foot.

1750–75

Chippendale. Mahogany, walnut, cherry.

1785–1800

Hepplewhite. Mahogany, much veneer.

1790–1820

Sheraton. Mahogany with satinwood; cherry with fancy maple.

1825–40

Empire. Mahogany, much veneer.

1830–68

Early Victorian. Mahogany, walnut, with many Belter pieces in rosewood.

1868–1900

Late Victorian. Oak, poplar, walnut, elm, birch, ash.

Apple

Looks like cherry but is lighter in color, streaked with thin curvy brown lines. Cuts smooth, but is too hard for carving.

Ash, white

Has gray tone with long straight grain. Hard as a baseball bat, good for bending, but uninteresting in texture and appearance.

Baywood, red

Used in southern pieces, is of the magnolia family, has miniature magnolia bloom when growing. In raw state, it is similar to low-grade mahogany and used mostly as a secondary wood.

Birch

Stains well, finishes better than maple and is heavier grain than maple. Often used to imitate cherry.

Butternut

Hard, close grained, finishes a very light brown. Finer in texture than white walnut. Even texture, good for carving and turning, harder and stronger than mahogany.

Cherry

Close grain, even texture, good for carving and turning. Harder and stronger than mahogany. Heavy when lifted. Reddish brown color when finished, with golden highlights. Wide boards often have yellow streaks at one side. This is known as sapwood. Walnut has same condition.

Chestnut

Tan, not as yellow as oak. Stained in Victorian furniture to look like oak or walnut. Doesn't warp. Used for frames, drawers and under veneer. Chestnut is distinctly American and is seldom found in furniture of any other country.

Gumwood, red

Fine grain, browner than cherry, same as sapwood. Hard to work, but polishes beautifully.

Mahogany

Honduras or American mahogany used until 1850s, after which it was imported from Africa. Philippine mahogany has larger pores than African and is lighter. Scrape bottom of drawer or table and wet to distinguish between the varieties. Older mahogany will be almost same color wet or dry. Philippine is rose toned, while African is in between the two.

Maple

Hard enough to bend your nail. Comes in plain grain tiger stripe (which comes from the crosswood) and bird's eye (which is formed from the sap). Tiger stripe is known as fiddleback in the South and curly maple in New England. Because of its strength, maple is used in chairs. New maple is almost white, but old maple is yellow or brownish yellow.

Oak

Doesn't change or warp, which is why fourteenth, fifteenth and sixteenth century oak furniture is still around. Oak has to be cured to carve. It's too hard for a chisel. You can't drive a nail into oak without using a drill. It yellows to any stain. Used in very early 1600s' furniture, it went out of fashion until the Victorian period when other woods became scarce.

Pine, white

Old pine is golden, amost poreless and grainless, with russet streaks. Dents easily. Favorite of early country wood-workers because it could be worked with hand tools. Usually not hard enough for chairs or table tops as it stains and marks easily.

Pine, yellow

Hard and golden with russet streaks. More common and plentiful from Virginia southward. Very sturdy and hardens with seasoning and age.

Poplar

Green and yellow streaked, very even in texture, but not as strong as pine, nor as durable, one reason you seldom see poplar floors. Has no distinctive grain, color or figure. Takes any color, so it is often used to piece and imitate other woods. Greeny tan heartwood.

Rosewood

Dark, purplish brown with black streaks. Came into use in Empire and Victorian periods. Used solid and for veneer.

Sycamore

Related to the buttonwood. Marvelous grain, used in decorative way.

Tulipwood

Used for inlay, comes from South Africa. Tan and pink with brown streaks. White when new, it ages to yellow and brownish yellow.

Walnut

Browner than mahogany, fine texture, easy to carve. Supply was exhausted during Victorian periods so manufacturers switched back to oak. The world's leading furniture wood when abundant and available, it is now scarce and expensive. Most present-day cuttings are being used for veneer.

CHAPTER 40

You

Antiques are fun. Some may not add up as blue-chip investments, but what they lack in breeding, they often make up for in personality. If an antique says something to you, don't worry what the experts think. Buy it and start a lifelong friendship.

It will never let you down. It can light up a room, start conversations in the unlikeliest places and introduce you to some of the nicest people you'll ever meet.

Unlike new furniture, it will always be worth more than you paid for it, easier to control as an investment than the stock market and faster to liquidate when you need ready cash.

Antiques don't lie. They can't.

Now that you know what they have been trying to tell you all these years, don't you think it's time you started listening?